The Great MANTRA for Mystic Meditation

The Great MANTRA for Mystic Meditation

Opening the Lotus of Good Fortune

Ūrmilā Devī Dāsī

First published in India by Lakshavedhi
Target Publication, 2012

Second Edition

Published by Padma Inc., 2013
Hillsborough, NC, USA

Printed by CreateSpace, An Amazon.com Company
Available from Amazon.com and other retail outlets

Design by Michael Best
Set in Cambria

"One's memory of Kṛṣṇa is revived by chanting the *mahā-mantra,* Hare Kṛṣṇa. By this practice of chanting and hearing the sound vibration of the Supreme Lord, one's ear, tongue and mind are engaged. This mystic meditation is very easy to practice, and it helps one attain the Supreme Lord."

A.C. Bhaktivedanta Swami Prabhupāda,
Bhagavad-gītā As It Is 8.8, Purport

Contents

Illustrators

Aṣṭasakhī-lila Devī Dāsī

Dynamic, Expanding Bliss: The Hare Kṛṣṇa Mantra
Concentration and Desire
The True Meaning and Glories of the Holy Name
Receiving and Giving the Holy Name
The Mood of Surrender
Progress to Pure Chanting

Śyāma Vallabhā Devī Dāsī

Respect for Those Who Give the Holy Name
Esteem for Sacred Writings
Whose Name Is God's Name?

Dinara Lukmanova

Regard for Devotees of the Lord

Jahnu Dāsa

Is Kṛṣṇa Our Master or Our Servant?

Elvira Lukmanova

Cover

CHAPTER 1

Dynamic, Expanding Bliss: The Hare Kṛṣṇa Mantra

Lord Kṛṣṇa's holy names bring light to downtown London on a Saturday night.

We cross Oxford Street with five *mṛdaṅga* drums, two loud and deep African drums, *karatāla* cymbals, an accordion, and an electric guitar. Our chanting party consists of over a hundred members, from so many countries and ethnic backgrounds that the diversity is startling. There are men in *dhotis,* in suits, and in jeans, women in saris, colorful dresses, and subdued business clothes. We race or dance down the street, singing as fast as we run, churning up waves of spiritual joy.

The lead singer wears a wireless microphone on his head, and one member of the group carries a loudspeaker in a backpack. The electric-guitar player has his own speaker. So many devotees respond to the lead singer's chanting that all the words of the great mantra for deliverance—Hare Kṛṣṇa, Hare Kṛṣṇa, Kṛṣṇa Kṛṣṇa, Hare Hare/ Hare Rāma, Hare Rāma, Rāma Rāma, Hare Hare—distinctly echo through the London streets.

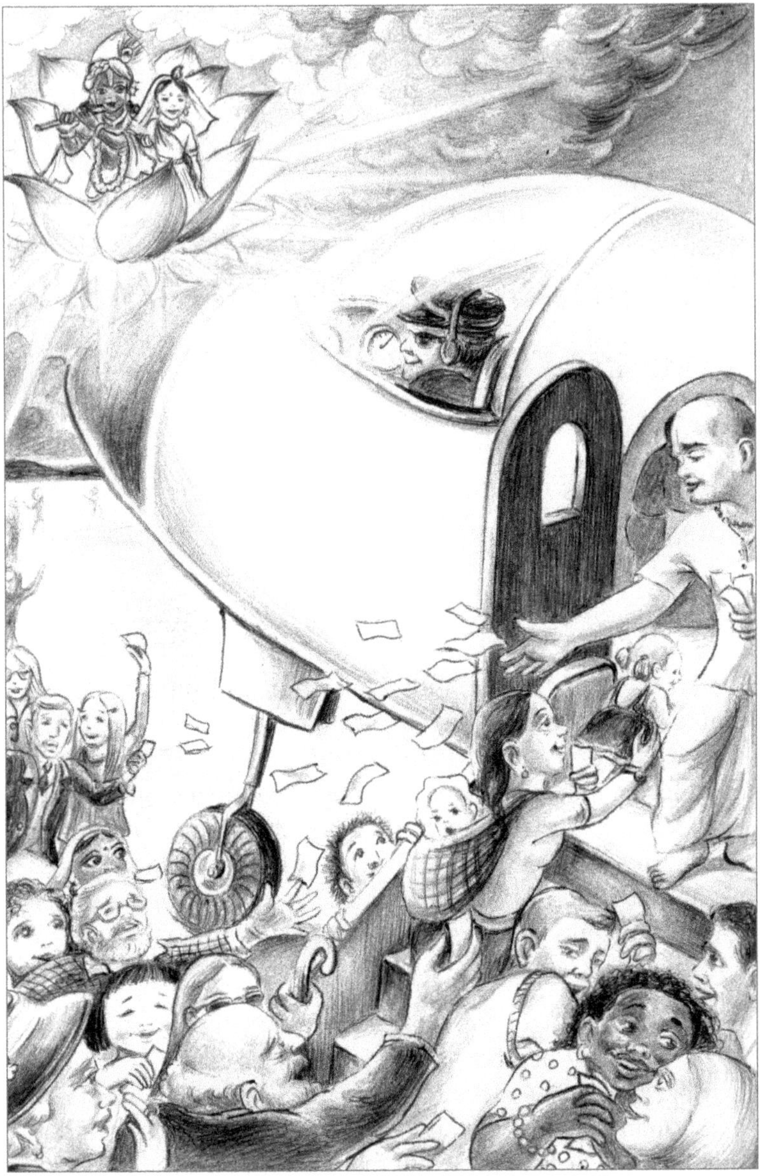

Chanting the Hare Kṛṣṇa mantra in public is like giving free tickets for everyone to travel to the spiritual world.

To this native New Yorker, the streets are narrow and the buildings short, but the atmosphere is that of any major Western city on a Saturday night. Many in the crowd must see us each week, but there are also large numbers of tourists and people who come from around the country to sample the culture of central London. And there is much to sample—pubs, gambling houses, live theater, movie houses with multiple screens, discotheques that open at 9:00 P.M., and shops of all variety.

But all the glitter of this great Western city, old with history and achievement, is, from the spiritual point of view, a subculture. The activities here, advertised by seductive models under flashing colored lights, draw humanity far away from the qualities that build a foundation for enlightenment, qualities that demarcate us as human. The people lining the streets are not thinking of enlightenment as they laugh in the outer darkness of night and the inner darkness of lust, greed, intoxication, and sensual enticements.

Spontaneous Dancing

Yet the chance for enlightenment comes. Our group randomly runs, jumps, and leaps across the streets, under archways, and even into the subway, where the acoustics intensify the chanting. In parks or streets closed to traffic, we linger for some time, sections of our group spontaneously performing dances that seem choreographed. An appreciative crowd gathers. I'm amazed by how many people join the dancing, carry our flags and banners for a while, sing with us, or simply smile, wave, or nod. I try to make eye contact with as many onlookers as possible, smiling and drawing them into the chanting. Hecklers appear, too, but their harsh condemnation drowns in our overflowing happiness and enthusiasm.

One man quietly tells me he has read *Bhagavad-gītā* but doesn't understand why there should be love and violence in a spiritual treatise. Alongside the chanters, we talk for a while about how God is the source of everything, including love and fighting. In God, Kṛṣṇa, these feelings and activities exist in their original, pure form. Reading or hearing of these will purify us from the base forms of lust and anger. Lust, anger, and greed are gates to suffering in this and future lives, but the spiritual originals, of which these are a twisted counterpart, are a source of varieties of great pleasure.

Some members of the party hand out books, magazines, or invitations to the next festival, but most of us are caught up in the mantra, the melody, and the movements that naturally express themselves in our bodies. We cannot help but dance. How can we dance and sing publicly with such abandon? Some onlookers probably assume we've been drinking, but we take no alcohol or other intoxicants and many of us are shy. Others only familiar with quiet personal meditation may be surprised that total absorption in a mantra would express itself as public exuberance. One member of the chanting party is out for the first time, nervously wondering if his boss is sitting at a restaurant window we pass. Perhaps some of us consider what people will think of our acting like madmen, but most of us are so absorbed in the chanting that public opinion seems like a far-away dream of no value.

The Great Call to God

The greatest mystery is the mantra itself, its meaning and power, and the effect on those of us who abandon ordinary decorum to sing it on busy streets. It is a prayer, a hymn, but of the greatest intensity and intimacy of all calls to God.

The mantra is a direct address: "O Kṛṣṇa, Supreme Lord, Absolute Truth, the most attractive person because of Your incomparable and unlimited beauty, wealth, fame, strength, intelligence, and renunciation! O Harā, Rādhā, female consort of the Lord, who steals His mind with love and takes away our material attachment and suffering! O Rāma, supreme reservoir of all pleasure, who enjoys transcendent love in Your own kingdom!"

What do we ask for when we call out to Kṛṣṇa and His supreme energy? Service. The mantra is a plea for loving service and for connection—yoga—in divine love.

We ask not for material wealth, fame, sensual and mental pleasure, or even salvation apart from serving Kṛṣṇa. As such, the mantra we sing with captivating melodies and expert musical accompaniment is the key to the highest levels of religious and spiritual understanding and experience. It embodies the summit of purity and ecstatic divine love. The mantra is composed of the names of God, and His name is more than blessed—it is God Himself in a form of utmost mercy. Additionally, hidden in the arrangement of the divine names is the most secret and intimate beatitude shared between Kṛṣṇa and His consort, Rādhā: Their meeting and blissfully anguished separation, only to meet and separate again.

The mantra is a plea for loving service and for connection in divine love.

Entering All Hearts

How is it that the Hare Kṛṣṇa *mahā-mantra*—which invokes supreme mystery and power and is the most secret inner truth of the Absolute Truth—appears from our mouths among the weekend revelers? To fully enter into the chanting of the *mahā-mantra*, to even be qualified to hear and chant it, would seem to be reserved for the most pure and austere of spiritual adepts. Yet the *mahā-mantra*, while containing essential truth generally revealed only to the most exalted saints, is a form of Kṛṣṇa so benevolent that it enters the hearts of even the most materialistic. The tipsy passerby who sings with us in his partying mood gets a seed of spiritual understanding. The people who nod and wave or merely hear start their journey to perfection.

Those of us for whom chanting the Hare Kṛṣṇa mantra is a way of life chant not only periodically on the street but daily in group singing and in quiet personal meditation. Indeed, the ripe fruit of perfection is to chant incessantly, the mantra becoming the essential part of one's life.

Cultivating the fruit is a science, from planting the seed to harvesting. An expert gardener in this spiritual science learns and practices the art of chanting Hare Kṛṣṇa, Hare Kṛṣṇa, Kṛṣṇa Kṛṣṇa, Hare Hare/ Hare Rāma, Hare Rāma, Rāma Rāma, Hare Hare to achieve the full effect expeditiously and without deviation.

The science requires expert guidance, a life of purity and goodness, a mood of self-surrender, and avoidance of pitfalls. The essence is to have a life where everything is done as an offering to Kṛṣṇa, with the help of a spiritual master to whom one has firmly committed. Such a life includes the regular study of scriptures such as the *Bhagavad-gītā* and the *Śrīmad-Bhāgavatam*, living in a holy place (or sanctifying one's home), and making intimate friendships with like-minded devotees.

The pitfalls are intoxication, illicit sex (sex should be only in marriage for procreation), gambling, and eating of meat, fish, or eggs. One should also avoid offending or displeasing the mantra, understanding that the mantra is the same as the person Kṛṣṇa and wants to be approached in a particular way.

Avoiding Offenses

The *Padma Purāṇa* lists the following offenses to the Lord's name: To offend devotees of the Lord, to consider Kṛṣṇa's name to be equal to that of an ordinary being (even a demigod), to disobey the spiritual master, to blaspheme scripture, to interpret the mantra in a mundane way, to think its glories are exaggerated, to intentionally sin with the idea that the mantra will purify one, to consider the chanting to be material piety, to tell the name's glories to the faithless, to chant without attention, and to chant without faith or while keeping material attachments.

By carefully applying both the positive and negative standards, an aspirant for entering eternal bliss and knowledge will achieve the result quickly, even in this life. But anyone, serious or not, can take pleasure in the surge of spiritual energy that transforms the streets when Kṛṣṇa's devotees share the best secret with the world.

Hard to Stop

Our large group gradually makes its way around Soho Square and back to the temple. Few people are on the streets here, and it's late for us, who rise well before the sun. Yet we cannot stop so easily. Someone is collecting the flags and banners, but the chanting continues to fill the street for a while. We remember how Lord Kṛṣṇa finds the greatest pleasure by appearing—as Śrī Caitanya Mahāprabhu—in the mood of His own devotee and chanting like this all night in the company of His associates. Regrettably, my body, made of bone, muscle, and blood, must rest. But I hope that Kṛṣṇa mercifully allows me one day to sing His name forever.

CHAPTER 2

Regard for Devotees of the Lord

To please Kṛṣṇa by chanting His names, we must also please His servants.

How to instantly win people's hearts? Point out the good qualities of their children, or even their pets. How to make people dislike you? Insult or harm someone dear to them. Similarly, the most grievous way to block the Lord's mercy is to have contempt or irreverence for those who love and serve Him, especially those sacrificing to teach others about spiritual life. If we offend Kṛṣṇa by insulting His dear sons and servants, we will fail to feel the ecstasy of love of God when we chant His holy names, as in the *mahā-mantra:* Hare Kṛṣṇa, Hare Kṛṣṇa, Kṛṣṇa Kṛṣṇa, Hare Hare/ Hare Rāma, Hare Rāma, Rāma Rāma, Hare Hare.

The logic is easy to understand: Why should Kṛṣṇa show us mercy—revealing that the taste of His name is concentrated sweet joy—when we are intolerant of others, serving them only the bitterness of criticism and fault-finding? Kṛṣṇa in the form of His name is the most merciful, certainly. But why should He give mercy to the merciless?

The *Skanda Purāṇa* lists six improper dealings with God's devotees that obstruct one's chanting: to kill a devotee, to blaspheme a devotee, to envy a devotee, to get angry at a devotee, to fail to offer respects or obeisances to a devotee, or to not feel joy upon seeing a devotee. (Vaiṣṇava authorities say that our joy should extend to practitioners of other genuine spiritual processes, to devotees who have done or said something to cause us grief, and to devotees who have struggled with varieties of material enticements.) Some of these six unwanted interactions involve our bodies, others our words, and yet others our attitudes and thoughts.

Qualifying for the Spiritual World

Learning to interact properly with Kṛṣṇa's servants is the key to entering His abode. In Kṛṣṇa's kingdom, the spiritual world, everything is alive. Water, buildings, furniture, and clumps of grass are all living beings, far more realized in love of God than most of the devoutly religious of this world. All souls there are absorbed in thoughts of Kṛṣṇa's name, form, qualities, and adventures, and all are in harmony not only with Kṛṣṇa but with each other. Dedication to Kṛṣṇa and His holy name is not enough to enter that abode. We require real love for Kṛṣṇa—a love that fills our hearts so that it overflows with similar love for all living beings, who are part of Him.

If instead of loving Kṛṣṇa's devotees, we offend them, we are unlikely to reach perfection in one life. Śrīla Prabhupāda writes in *The Nectar of Devotion* (Chapter 18), "If it is seen that a person has developed a high standard of devotion without having undergone even the regulative principles, it is to be understood that his status of devotional service was achieved in a former life. For some reason or another it had been temporarily stopped, most probably by an offense committed at the lotus feet of a devotee. Now, with a good second chance, it has again begun to develop."

Caitanya Mahāprabhu explains that the effect of vilifying a devotee is similar to that of letting a wild elephant into a garden—one's spiritual progress is trampled. Unfortunately, a prime symptom of a neophyte, whose ignorance impedes his or her service to God, is mistreatment of other living beings. The beginner's lack of universal love and respect is evident in many sectarian religions. Congregations that show much reverence to God in their house of worship may exuberantly condemn all others who serve the same God in a different way. Going so far as to torture, persecute, or wage war against those whose rituals differ from theirs, such separatists displease Kṛṣṇa and sully the very concept of religion in the minds of innocent people.

Learning to interact properly with Kṛṣṇa's servants is the key to entering His abode.

What Can We Do?

Understanding the danger of criticizing God's devotees, then, and desiring full benefit from our chanting, we may resolve to feel joy upon seeing or hearing about others who love, or aspire to love, the Supreme Lord. We may resolve not to look for faults or think ourselves superior. Yet time and again, our mind may induce us to slam against this most formidable of blocks to self-realization. What can we do?

First, we can avoid intimate friendship with people who will encourage us to fault religious people. Rather, we can choose as close associates those free from the propensity to criticize others. When teaching about Kṛṣṇa consciousness, we may have to point out the flaws in a more elementary system of spiritual advancement, but we can still hold out all encouragement and love to those within that system. Our critique can be practical and constructive, without envy or hatred. And while we must carefully choose our intimates—selecting those most realized in spiritual science—we must mentally respect even the weakest who desire pure love of God.

Respect for Other Systems

It's easy to come up with excuses for criticizing and finding fault with others who are doing their best to serve the Supreme Lord. But if we consider who is guiding them and why these guides teach as they do, we'll see that our criticism is unfair. Sometimes the most exalted saint teaches in a circumstance where only lesser truth can be communicated, acting like a graduate professor teaching six-year-olds. We should remember that everyone needs to progress from his or her present position. So why fault the students or teachers in a religious system that teaches less than the highest knowledge and process? Rather than criticize beginning students, we should encourage and praise their attempt to love God. How happy the holy name is to know that we extend love and hope to those with less understanding or knowledge than ourselves! Is not criticizing them simply self-righteousness and pride, perhaps envy? Of course, we can honestly evaluate systems of religious and spiritual practice, as much as we can distinguish between primary school and doctoral programs. But we should remember that today's primary students might achieve doctoral degrees, while some now in graduate programs might fail to persevere.

Is it safe to point out genuine defects in others striving for perfection? The monk Thomas a Kempis addresses this question in the thirteenth-century work *Imitation of Christ*:

> Try to bear patiently with the defects and infirmities of others, whatever they may be, because you also have many a fault which others must endure. If you cannot make yourself what you wish to be, how can you bend others to your will? We want them to be perfect, yet we do not correct our own faults. We wish them to be severely corrected, yet we will not correct ourselves. Their great liberty displeases us, yet we would not be denied what we ask. We would have them bound by laws, yet we will allow ourselves to be restrained in nothing. Hence, it is clear how seldom we think of others as we do of ourselves.

In this connection, the great *Bhāgavatam* commentator Śrīdhara Svāmī wrote, "Whether the words are true or not, pointing out the faults of a Vaiṣṇava constitutes blasphemy."

Even if we meet a perfect, pure devotee who openly follows and teaches the principles at the pinnacle of spiritual life, we might find faults with his or her birth, background, past sins, unintentional sins, or traces of past sins. We might see a lack of some saintly qualities—kindness, peacefulness, truthfulness, magnanimity, cleanliness, and so on. But in time, full devotion to Kṛṣṇa will certainly bring out these qualities. Just because some are developing gradually, we shouldn't dwell on their current deficiency.

Begging Forgiveness

If despite our best efforts to cultivate respect and admiration for devotees of the Lord we instead offend them, we should lament, fall at their feet, and satisfy them with praise and respect. We should serve any unforgiving devotee for many days. If he or she continues to be angry with us, we should spend our time constantly chanting Kṛṣṇa's holy name.

It is important to fall at the feet of a devotee we've offended, even if that devotee has no quarrel with our words,

A devotee of the Lord will forgive offenses, but the dust from the devotee's feet may not forgive, and the offender may, therefore, suffer a reaction.

thoughts, or behavior. Such humble dealings will purify us and please Kṛṣṇa, who is much more unhappy with an offense to His devotees than to Himself. It is said that without falling at the devotee's feet, the devotee may forgive but the dust of his or her feet will hold one accountable. Performing a physical act of repentance when asking for forgiveness shows great humility and sincerity.

Just as Kṛṣṇa is the heartfelt friend of all living beings, one who wants to be His devotee should be a vehicle for revealing that friendship. A lover of God should love everyone who loves God. As we deal with Kṛṣṇa's devotees with reverence, the holy name will gradually show His full power. Then chanting Hare Kṛṣṇa will bring us to spiritual health, and we will know that there is nothing greater than the name, anywhere or at any time.

CHAPTER 3

Concentration and Desire

Chanting the Lord's name with full attention removes hindrances to pure chanting.

One day I sat with a group of friends, speaking of the day's business. Some other people walked by, and one of my friends thought he heard his name.

"Did you mention me?" he asked the passersby.

"No, we said something else," they replied.

Disappointed, he turned back to our conversation.

I thought of how when we are in a crowded room, others' conversation becomes a background buzz, but if our name is spoken, somehow we distinguish it and become alert.

Kṛṣṇa also is interested when it seems we're calling Him.

"Oh, do you want Me?" he asks.

But if we really said something else, or if we said His name carelessly, He will wait until we truly want Him. Therefore Śrīla Prabhupāda writes and speaks about chanting the Hare Kṛṣṇa mantra with quality. To take a vow to meet a quota of chanting is certainly valuable—simply doing so

When we chant with attention, Kṛṣṇa Himself is attracted.

shows spiritual sincerity—but the quality must be there as well. For beginners, making our quota may seem enough of a challenge. Still, we must progress to chanting that is a true call to the Lord.

When we chant with attention and in a mood of surrender and devotion, Kṛṣṇa naturally reciprocates with us. Then we quickly overcome all other obstacles to chanting, to spiritual life in general, and to our goal of perfect love for God. But if our chanting is without attention, all the hindrances will remain, if not increase.

Why is attentive chanting the key to being free from all other offenses to the name? When we chant with attention, we are in touch with Kṛṣṇa, who will then show us how, for example, we are dealing with other devotees with less than respect.

The root of inattention is distraction, or having an interest in something other than the name we are saying. This interest can be in wealth, material success, the opposite sex, position in society, or so many other things. Chanting with distraction is like asking someone a question and then thinking of other things, maybe even looking out the window, when they respond.

Besides basic distraction, chanting is inattentive if one is lazy—one's sluggish mind keeps stopping its focus on the name. We can also just be indifferent to the name, which from a spiritual point of view is madness—how can a sane person not value the holy name?

When we chant with attention and in a mood of surrender and devotion, Kṛṣṇa naturally reciprocates with us.

Aids to Attentive Chanting

To chant with care and attention, we should first be attentive to completing a fixed number of Hare Kṛṣṇa mantras daily. Any initiated disciple in the International Society for Krishna Consciousness must chant at least 1,728 mantras daily (16 times around the string of 108 beads), but beginners can start with any number, as long as there is steadiness. Steady, regular service is appreciated in any section of society; in spiritual life it is a sign of sincerity and devotion to the path.

To chant with full concentration, it is best to chant in a peaceful place. The best places are sheltered from material influence. One can chant in a temple, a sacred place of Kṛṣṇa's pastimes, or any quiet, secluded spot. One's home can be a temple, if Kṛṣṇa's deity and Kṛṣṇa's pleasure are made the center of life. The Hare Kṛṣṇa movement has many temples for public worship and education. In India, numerous traditional temples are devoted to Lord Kṛṣṇa, many at places where the He incarnated, displaying His divine activities.

Chanting with persons advanced in spiritual understanding helps too. Laziness will flee if our friends are those who eagerly absorb their consciousness in chanting, without wasting time in useless diversions. Naturally, in their company we will also imbibe a sense of urgency and determination.

It helps to chant at a quiet time (early morning is ideal). An inner mood of begging for Kṛṣṇa's mercy is also essential. These remedies will soon vanquish our insane indifference to the holy name.

A Wish for Millions of Mouths

To deal with the foundation of inattention—interest in something other than Kṛṣṇa and His name—it is wise to have times when we do nothing other than chant day and night. If on a holy day such as Ekādaśī* or the anniversary of Kṛṣṇa's appearance we abstain from eating, sleeping, ordinary business, and so on, and simply chant for hours without interruption, gradually our mind will rejoice in Kṛṣṇa. Such times of total absorption will aid our concentration on ordinary days of chanting.

Having conquered distraction, laziness, and inattention, we will chant, as Prabhupāda says, like a child calling its mother—with great intensity, desire, and helplessness.

When our chanting is with full concentration of mind and heart, we will never find it boring, nor will we need to give much care to the stumbling blocks that trip so many on the path to perfection. The blocks will melt into the road, making our way easy and expeditious. Then, like the great teacher Rūpa Gosvāmī, we will say, "I do not know how much nectar the two syllables 'Kṛṣ-ṇa' have produced. When the holy name of Kṛṣṇa is chanted, it appears to dance within the mouth. We then desire many, many mouths. When that name enters the holes of the ears, we desire many millions of ears. And when the holy name dances in the courtyard of the heart, it conquers the activities of the mind, and therefore all the senses become inert."

---

* Ekādaśī occurs twice each lunar month, on the eleventh day of both the waxing and waning moon. Spiritual progress is easier on Ekādaśī, a day dedicated to worship of Lord Kṛṣṇa. To put full energy into chanting and serving Kṛṣṇa, His devotees fast from grains and beans (heavy foods) on Ekādaśī, or even from food, water, and sleep.

CHAPTER 4

Is Kṛṣṇa Our Master or Our Servant?

Because Kṛṣṇa's name has immense spiritual power, we must be careful how we use it.

The students of my Government class and I sat hushed, without even rustling papers, listening to the amazing story in the courtroom. At least it amazed these fifteen- and sixteen-year-old students whose lives never touched those of drug addicts and criminals.

"You've broken your probation three times," the stern judge said. He leaned forward on the desk and glared at the man in shackles and bright orange prison clothes. "You've had to go to a drug-rehabilitation program. Each time you start the program, but then you leave. Do you know the penalty for breaking probation?"

The young accused—with muscular arms and a nearly shaved head—stood straight like a soldier and said nothing. He almost succeeded in appearing repentant. At least the judge might have thought so.

"Fifteen years," the words came heavily and slowly. "Fifteen years. Back in prison for fifteen years." There was a long pause. "Do you want to go back to prison for fifteen years?"

"No, your honor. I just hated that treatment program I was sentenced to. I'd like a chance at another kind of program. Please. One last chance. If it's the program I'm asking for, I'll definitely stick with it and kick this cocaine for good."

The court reporter held her fingers above the keys. No one moved.

"Okay," the judge said, still leaning forward with his full weight on his arms. We all realized we hadn't breathed for a minute or so. Now a cough, now a shuffle.

"But this is your last chance!" the judge almost spat out, and we either slightly jumped or suddenly leaned forward. "You cannot keep breaking probation and asking for another chance. This is it. Make it good."

He broke eye contact and turned to the papers on his desk. "Next case."

And the prisoner left to complete the procedures.

Kṛṣṇa, the Merciful Judge

Was this criminal ready for reformation? Or was he just using the judge's mercy to try to cheat the system? We didn't follow up on the case, but we doubted the young man's motives.

Like the judge, Kṛṣṇa and saintly persons, including the guru who takes responsibility to bring us to Kṛṣṇa, are happy to forgive our mistakes, even grievous sins. But what if we deliberately use the Lord, His servants, or any aspect of His service—especially the chanting of His name—to get relief from sins? Then Kṛṣṇa will cease His leniency and block our

Some people think if they give stolen money to a religious person they will not have to suffer for stealing.

realization of Him, because we're trying to engage Him as our servant.

In 1992, Charles H. Keating, Jr., was found guilty of stealing over a quarter of a billion dollars through fraud. He gave at least a million dollars of this, much taken from others' life savings, to Mother Teresa to help the poor of Calcutta. The District Attorney who prosecuted Mr. Keating wrote to Mother Teresa asking her to give the donation back to the crime victims.

"It is not uncommon for 'con' men to be generous with family, friends and charities," the District Attorney wrote. "Perhaps they believe that their generosity will purchase love, respect or forgiveness. However, the time when the purchase of 'indulgences' as an acceptable method of seeking forgiveness died with the Reformation. No church, no charity, no organization should allow itself to be used as salve for the conscience of the criminal."

The District Attorney was referring to the Protestant Reformation, which was largely fueled by objection to "indulgences," where in exchange for donations the Church would promise remission of punishment for sin.

The mentality of using religion or spiritual practice to avoid punishment is often called the worst offense to the Lord; it blocks our spiritual progress. Śrīla Prabhupāda termed this offense, when applied to the chanting of the Lord's holy name, "sinning on the strength of chanting." There is no remedy if a person schemes to defraud the Lord in this way. One who thinks "I'll do this bad thing and then chant Hare Kṛṣṇa to be excused" will find that Kṛṣṇa will put obstacles on his or her path, especially if the sin or crime was done against the Lord's devotee.

Generally, if a person is constantly serving Kṛṣṇa and chanting Hare Kṛṣṇa, Hare Kṛṣṇa, Kṛṣṇa Kṛṣṇa, Hare Hare/

Hare Rāma, Hare Rāma, Rāma Rāma, Hare Hare, the very process of chanting and performing other service to Kṛṣṇa will gradually render offenses and sins ineffective. But if one takes advantage of the protection offered by chanting, one's chanting will remain just alphabet sounds—Kṛṣṇa will not manifest Himself there.

Defining "Sin"

What, exactly, do we mean by "sin," and is there a difference between deliberate and accidental sin?

Some definitions Śrīla Prabhupāda gives us are "breaking the laws of nature," "deepening involvement in the complexities of material nature," and doing something that "leads us away from the Supreme Lord." Once we understand that our most essential nature is loving service to Kṛṣṇa, anything other than that, or anything opposed to it, is sin. Sin isn't exactly something bad that God doesn't want you to do because He's a cruel rule-enforcer, but it's something that causes misery because it's against one's very self.

For example, the nature of the human body is to digest organic material, especially fruits, grains, vegetables, and so forth. If we choose to eat Styrofoam, we do something against the nature or "law" of the body and will therefore suffer. Similarly, anything we think, say, or do that doesn't nourish our love for Kṛṣṇa is spiritually indigestible and brings the pain of material involvement, which is disease for the soul.

A person whose consciousness is in disharmony with Kṛṣṇa may not know, however, what is and is not in accordance with spiritual reality. Therefore bona fide scripture lists condemned acts that require atonement. These acts—of the body, mind, or speech—are sins.

Certainly one who hasn't attained the pinnacle of purity is living in an interim state between sin and a pure life. While striving for purity, we retain mental impressions of sin and a strong tendency to use the body, mind, and words in ways that take us away from Kṛṣṇa. Śrīla Viśvanātha Cakravartī Ṭhākura writes in *Mādhurya Kadambinī,* "Seeing that material enjoyment is forcibly carrying him away and impairing his steadiness in serving Kṛṣṇa, the devotee resolves to renounce his addictions and take shelter of the holy name. But many times the attempt at renunciation ends in enjoying what he is trying to renounce."

Striving to Improve

This struggle with our persistent tendency to turn away from Kṛṣṇa is not a block if we continually take up the challenge to improve. Kṛṣṇa explains: "Having awakened faith in topics about Me, My devotee is disgusted with all material activities, knowing that sense gratification leads to misery. Still, though he tries he is unable to give up his material desires and sometimes engages in the same sense enjoyment that brings only misery. But, repenting such activities, he should worship Me with love, faith, and firm conviction." (*Śrīmad-Bhāgavatam* 11.20.27–28)

Śrīla Prabhupāda writes: "An ordinary man with firm faith in the eternal injunctions of the Lord, even though unable to execute such orders, becomes liberated from the bondage of the law of karma. In the beginning of Kṛṣṇa consciousness, one may not fully discharge the injunctions of the Lord, but because one is not resentful of this principle and works sincerely without consideration of defeat and hopelessness, he will surely be promoted to the stage of pure Kṛṣṇa consciousness." (*Bhagavad-gītā As It Is* 3.31, Purport)

Minor sins that we commit as we struggle to advance are considered accidental. By repentance we should burn the reaction to those sins. But if we sin thinking that either ordinary religious penance or transcendental activities such as chanting will deliver us from the reaction, the reaction will increase rather than decrease.

If a person externally takes on the appearance of a religious or saintly person while still secretly doing materialistic activities for sense pleasure, such behavior is also sinning on the strength of chanting. There are more subtle aspects as well. For example, we may think, "I'm a devotee of Kṛṣṇa and please Him in so many ways. If I just do this little thing wrong, surely He'll overlook it."

For our chanting to have full effect, therefore, we must throw out the cheating tendency if it even sticks its toenail into the doorway of our mind. If we find ourselves planning to use Kṛṣṇa and His name to cover our devious purposes, we should strongly call to Kṛṣṇa for protection. Our gurus—both the one who has initiated us into the chanting and those who give us relevant spiritual instruction—are our guardians and will also chase away the thieves of sin and cheating if we loudly and strongly beg for their help.

A remedy for all obstacles is the regular, close companionship of pure devotees of Kṛṣṇa. Their examples and teachings help us recognize our difficulties and desire to be free of them.

Of course, we want not only to be free of the desire to use chanting to cheat our way out of suffering for sin, but to give up our sinful tendency completely. Only a pure life fully in harmony with the truth of our spiritual nature will give us the satisfaction we are always seeking. And only a pure life will prepare the ground for the garden that will grow the flowers and fruits of love of God.

We will never sin if we have contempt for the illusion of material enjoyment. Part of that contempt will arise naturally if we have the superior pleasure of serving Kṛṣṇa. At the same time, we should study the true nature of material life from scriptures and saintly persons. The root of sin is ignorance, or ignoring the obvious truths of what it really means to turn away from Kṛṣṇa. The results of sin are birth, death, old age, and disease. One will never be satisfied with the pleasures of the body and mind separated from Kṛṣṇa, and even things that apparently satisfy for a time will quickly fade, being temporary by nature. Why delight in what is temporary and superficial? Such delight is the true nature of sin.

Kṛṣṇa's Protection

Kṛṣṇa as Rāma promises, "It is My vow that if one only once seriously surrenders unto Me, saying 'My dear Lord, from this day I am Yours,' and prays to Me for courage, I shall immediately award courage to that person, and he will always remain safe from that time on." (*Rāmāyaṇa, Yuddha-khaṇḍa* 18.33) From what is one safe? Kṛṣṇa says, "Just surrender unto Me. I shall deliver you from all sinful reactions. Do not fear." (*Bhagavad-gītā* 18.66) Those sinful reactions include the very desire—even potential desire—to sin.

And how do we surrender? We accept whatever will help us in spiritual life and reject what will be harmful. We learn from scriptures, gurus, and saintly persons what will be favorable or unfavorable. We see that ultimately only Kṛṣṇa is our protector and maintainer, and we are happily willing to put His interest as our interest. And no matter what our qualifications and achievements, we give Kṛṣṇa the credit, remaining humble.

This mood of surrender will quickly vanquish our tendency to sin and to misuse the holy name to cheat. It will allow the power and beauty of the name to blossom in our hearts.

CHAPTER 5

The True Meaning and Glories of the Holy Name

We risk disrespecting God when we undervalue the spiritual power of chanting His names.

"She has between two and twenty-four hours left."

My mother's breathing had become labored, and she could no longer give that tiny nod or shake of head to indicate her desires.

So, it had come. Unable to speak, my mother had written "When?" once or twice in her many weeks without any sustenance but water. Now I immediately thought of rituals of protection—marking her body with sacred clay, putting beads of *tulasī* wood on her, and so on. But that was not to be.

"No Kṛṣṇa rituals," my cousin the doctor admonished me. Although not her attending physician, being a doctor he had more or less taken charge of things. "Your mother was not a Hare Kṛṣṇa. Let her die as she lived."

"But," I argued, "these last weeks I've been chanting to her, reading stories to her from our scriptures, singing devotional songs. She often asked me to, and really loved it. Why should I do something different today?"

I was hopeful, yet nervous. For two weeks now I'd been with my mother twelve hours or more a day. The first week my muscles gradually became intensely strained, as I was on constant full alert, trying to notice when death would come so I could help her remember Kṛṣṇa. Finally I understood: If I told my mother to surrender to Kṛṣṇa, I had to do the same. The time and circumstances of her death were not in my hands. I couldn't be with her every moment, controlling the situation. Hadn't her roommate here in the nursing home, apparently in reasonably good condition, died unexpectedly from a heart attack practically in this very room just days ago? At that moment, I'd been at the nurses' station. Would I be there when my mother's death came?

"No Kṛṣṇa rituals," he repeated.

I sighed and then looked directly into his eyes and shook his hand.

"No rituals," I said, "and that's a promise."

Keeping that promise, I again read my mother the story of how Kṛṣṇa married Rukmiṇī. Then I chanted out loud on my beads, "Hare Kṛṣṇa, Hare Kṛṣṇa, Kṛṣṇa Kṛṣṇa, Hare Hare/ Hare Rāma, Hare Rāma, Rāma Rāma, Hare Hare."

My mother's private aide, who had worked as a registered nurse in South America, was an educated, intelligent woman with a sweet simple faith in God and Jesus.

When she heard my chanting, she said with a conspiratorial glance, "Your cousin is still in the building."

When he returned to the room sometime later, I quickly put down my beads, but though he saw and heard me chanting, he didn't complain. Did he understand that chanting the holy name is not a religious ritual, what to speak of a sectarian one?

Purity Without Rituals

Because Kṛṣṇa, the Supreme Lord, is the summit and definition of purity, no one can achieve His direct service without also being pure. All the genuine scriptures and religious traditions of the world, therefore, have rituals and processes for bringing a human being to a level of purity where love of God becomes possible. But the holy name itself has the power to create purity without the need of rituals.

Unfortunately, transcendent spiritual practices such as chanting God's names can be mistaken for rituals or become transformed into external, meaningless traditions over time. Therefore, many people assume that the chanting of Kṛṣṇa's names, as in Hare Kṛṣṇa, Hare Kṛṣṇa, Kṛṣṇa Kṛṣṇa, Hare Hare/ Hare Rāma, Hare Rāma, Rāma Rāma, Hare Hare, is the formal procedure of a particular religious sect, meant for gaining worldly happiness, power over the body and mind, or salvation. Such thinking is an offense to the name. Similar offenses are to give a material interpretation of the holy name and to think that the spiritual glories attributed to the name are exaggerations or mythology. If we offend the name in these ways, Kṛṣṇa will hide His name's true meaning and blessings from us. The result will be sorrow, rather than the awakening of our love for Kṛṣṇa.

There are reasons why we might be confused about the transcendental nature of Kṛṣṇa's name. For example, the scriptures promise material rewards or liberation to one who chants the holy name. And there are standard procedures—apparently rituals—for chanting the Lord's name, such as taking a vow to chant a certain number of names a day and using beads as an aid to meditation.

Kṛṣṇa's name, however, is Kṛṣṇa Himself incarnated as sound. The holy name comes directly from the most intimate, sacred realm of the Supreme: Goloka Vṛndāvana, Kṛṣṇa's abode in the spiritual world. The holy name is Kṛṣṇa entering our hearts and rising to dance on our tongues. But just as computer novices know only a few elementary functions, beginners in spiritual science may not appreciate who the name is and how the name is within their mouth. In other words, beginners might not understand that the holy name has unlimited power.

Kṛṣṇa has invested the holy name with all energies, so chanting gives one access to all energies, including the spiritual. In contrast, a person who performs mundane, karmic activities, or pious acts meant to obtain wealth, health, and other things of this world, contacts only material energies. And meditation, contemplation, and philosophical endeavors connect one only with energies for salvation, sometimes called *brahma-nirvāṇa.* Therefore, we offend the name if we think chanting to be only as potent as activities of piety and salvation.

The holy name comes directly from Goloka Vṛndāvana, the most intimate, sacred realm of the Supreme.

It is true that sometimes working piously (karma) or for liberation (through *jñāna*) helps create a situation conducive to chanting the holy name. Yet the difference between these activities and chanting can be further explained as follows. Actions for piety or salvation are means to an end. They're eventually abandoned and are always less than pure. Chanting the holy name, however, is both the principal means to attain love of God and the main activity one performs once one attains that love. The holy name is never impure; the purity and glories of the name become uncovered as the chanter's purity increases. A person who understands these points about the holy name rejects karma and *jñāna* and takes solely to *bhakti*, which centers on chanting.

Works and Faith

Critics of chanting who see it as a ritual say that God and His service are unattainable through our own effort, including chanting. Like austerities, study, and other "works" (to use the biblical term), chanting can't force God to accept us. We would agree with that—at least in the sense of mechanical chanting. Śrīla Prabhupāda writes, "Revival of the dormant affection or love of Godhead does not depend on the mechanical system of hearing and chanting, but it solely and wholly depends on the causeless mercy of the Lord. When the Lord is fully satisfied with the sincere efforts of the devotee, He may endow him with His loving transcendental service." (*Śrīmad-Bhāgavatam* 1.7.6, Purport)

What are those "sincere efforts" that attract the grace of Kṛṣṇa? They are our efforts to grab Kṛṣṇa's merciful love when offered. The externals of genuine systems of spiritual life and religion, such as taking up a regime of chanting, are meant to display our sincerity to Kṛṣṇa so that He will be inclined to reveal Himself to us.

There is thus a symbiosis between "works" and "faith" (citing the biblical terms again). But ordinary pious or philanthropic works do not attract Kṛṣṇa's attention, although they can be helpful to bring a soul to a life of self-realization. Only work in devotion, in direct service to the Lord and saintly persons, brings Kṛṣṇa's notice.

In fact, ultimately nothing but the mercy of the Lord will bring us to our original state of spiritual happiness.

There are faults in every material activity, even religious rituals, just as fire produces smoke. Chanting the Lord's name, however, is simply full of bliss

The main way to show our desire for this mercy is to connect with Kṛṣṇa's names, especially by chanting the *mahā-mantra:* Hare Kṛṣṇa, Hare Kṛṣṇa, Kṛṣṇa Kṛṣṇa, Hare Hare/ Hare Rāma, Hare Rāma, Rāma Rāma, Hare Hare.

But what of those material benefits promised to the chanter? They're true, and not held up as merely glittering trinkets to attract our attention and get our motivation churning. Yet Kṛṣṇa's devotee may not achieve such benefits. Why? Because the devotee doesn't ask for those small and tasteless fruits, having attained the juicy sweet nectar of Kṛṣṇa's love.

The scriptures also describe examples of immediate tremendous spiritual realization and purification through chanting and other transcendent services of devotion. Because such results are uncommon, however, one might think the scriptures exaggerate the benefits of chanting. But the benefits are real. It's just a matter of when and how a person experiences the name's glories, and that depends on Kṛṣṇa's mercy and the chanter's careful avoidance of offenses.

Why Chanting Gives Happiness

Some people think that positive changes in one who chants the holy names result from the mechanics of chanting rather than from a spiritual transformation. For example, a prominent American newsmagazine recently ran a cover article about how all "religious experience" can be attributed to the brain's neurological functions. In other words, some scientists claim that the physical act of chanting changes brain chemistry and such alterations cause what is then termed spiritual happiness or realization. But scriptures and saints tell us that transcendent pleasure and understanding cause positive changes in the body and mind, some of which may be measured in brain chemistry. It is reasonable that the love of someone enraptured by Kṛṣṇa would affect the body in which he or she resides, just as a party in a house would vibrate the walls and floors. To state that the floors' vibrations caused the joyous mood of the revelers would be illogical.

The holy name has the potency to transform someone from illusioned to enlightened because the name is Kṛṣṇa Himself and in the form of the *mahā-mantra*—Hare Kṛṣṇa, Hare Kṛṣṇa, Kṛṣṇa Kṛṣṇa, Hare Hare/ Hare Rāma, Hare Rāma, Rāma Rāma, Hare Hare —it is the Lord and His supreme energy, Rādhā. The word *Hare* is the way to call someone named either Hari (masculine, a name for Kṛṣṇa) or Harā (feminine, a name for Rādhārāṇī). Śrīla Prabhupāda told us that we are calling to the supreme mother, Harā, to help us approach the Lord, Kṛṣṇa or Rāma. Kṛṣṇa means all-attractive, an appropriate name for God because He is the strongest and the most wealthy, renounced, famous, beautiful, and intelligent—the primary categories of opulence. And Rāma is a name for God as the supreme enjoyer, full of pleasure. *Harā* literally means "to take away." Rādhārāṇī, addressed as Hare, takes away the pain of material attachments and brings us to Kṛṣṇa. She also steals Kṛṣṇa's mind, attracting the most attractive with her incomparable love. The *mahā-mantra* is thus an exultation of Rādhā-Kṛṣṇa's love and a plea to Rādhā-Kṛṣṇa to allow the chanter to help further the unlimited expansion of Their love.

Many great spiritual teachers have given their own meditations on the name and the *mahā-mantra,* all in accord with the basic understanding above. Bhaktivinoda Ṭhākura, for example, explained that each couplet of the mantra refers to one of the eight prayers (*Śikṣāṣṭaka*) written by the Lord to Himself when, as Caitanya Mahāprabhu, He appeared in the mood of Rādhārāṇī. Bhaktivinoda further says that each of these couplets and prayers corresponds to a stage in the gradual progress of realization of a spiritual aspirant.

"Go to Govinda!"

Kṛṣṇa may find many ways to convince us of the name's power. My mother's passing was a powerful lesson for me.

My many relatives who had vehemently objected to "Kṛṣṇa rituals," both directly and through the doctor, suddenly and inexplicably left the room after declaring that they would stay "until the end." As I sat with my mother, another devotee entered the room and began chanting Hare Kṛṣṇa to her, not knowing she had only moments left.

The aide sat on one side, saying, "Just go to the Lord, just love the Lord!" And I sat on the other, describing Kṛṣṇa's form and singing songs of the spiritual world. My mother's body shuddered as if someone had grabbed the stem of a large plant within her and shaken it. For several weeks, she'd been unable to speak, even though her consciousness had been clear and alert. Was it her inner desire that had set the stage for hearing only Kṛṣṇa's glories? Would my relatives come back and accuse me of sectarian rituals? Would she go on like this for days, with the chance that I could be out of the room at the moment the soul left? Leaving all this up to Kṛṣṇa, I told her of His beautiful hair, His eyes, and His love.

"Go to Govinda! Go to Gopāla! Give Him all your love and everything. Leave your material attachments and become attached only to Him. *Rādhe Jaya Jaya, Mādhava.* Go to Gopāla!"

Her breathing stopped. Then a tiny bit of air came from her mouth, and her body was still. Could one whose life had no background of Vedic ritual come to Kṛṣṇa through the power of His name, even in the last moments? I'm still astonished at how the holy name is so merciful and how Kṛṣṇa in that form is above all considerations.

The phone rang.

"How is Grandma?" my daughter asked.

"Grandma just died. One minute ago."

"One minute ago? One minute ago I was at the altar, begging Lord Caitanya to protect her."

With faith in the power of the name, with awareness that Kṛṣṇa in that form is fully present with all potencies, and with conviction that the names includes and is beyond all else, let us chant with enthusiasm.

The Glory Of Chanting

"There is no vow like chanting the holy name, no knowledge superior to it, no meditation that comes anywhere near it. It gives the highest result. No penance is equal to it, and nothing is as powerful as the holy name.

"Chanting is the greatest act of piety and the supreme refuge. Even the words of the *Vedas* do not possess enough power to describe its magnitude. Chanting is the highest path to liberation, peace, and eternal life. It is the pinnacle of devotion, the heart's joyous proclivity and attraction, and the best form of remembrance of the Supreme Lord. The holy name has appeared solely for the benefit of the living entities as their lord and master, their supreme worshipful object, and their spiritual guide and mentor.

"In spite of the influences of Kali-yuga, whoever continuously chants Lord Kṛṣṇa's holy name, even in sleep, can easily realize that the name is a direct manifestation of Kṛṣṇa Himself."

—Śrīla Bhaktivinoda Ṭhākura, *Śaraṇāgati* (quoted from *Agni Purāṇa*)

CHAPTER 6

Respect for Those Who Give the Holy Name

Lord Kṛṣṇa reveals Himself through His holy names to chanters who honor and obey His agents.

The celestial city Indrapurī is the residence of Indra, one of the *devas* who manage universal affairs in service to the Supreme Lord, Kṛṣṇa. In Indrapurī the scent of smoke from *aguru* incense mixes with the fragrance of flowers that decorate the parks and the bodies of the residents. Strings of natural pearls adorn the buildings, and benches carved from diamond and coral line the spotless roadways. Indrapurī is off limits to the sinful, cunning, lusty, greedy, envious, violent, or falsely proud.

Indra's wife, Śacī, sits beside him on his throne, as the dancers and singers of this material heaven entertain them with music glorifying Kṛṣṇa. A white umbrella that glows like the moon is Indra's royal canopy.

Although Indra is a powerful *deva,* his enemies, the *asuras* (demons), were once able to attack his heavenly kingdom

Absorbed in entertainment, the heavenly kind Indra ignored his guru.

and injure him and his associates. Because of disrespecting his spiritual master, Indra had become vulnerable.

Once, while enjoying his wealth and power on his jeweled throne, Indra saw Bṛhaspati, his guru, enter the palace hall. According to etiquette, Indra should have stood to greet him with a seat, sweet words, and some refreshment. But because Indra was used to seeing Bṛhaspati every day, he ignored him. Offended, Bṛhaspati left.

Indra quickly understood his omission and took to the standard method of rectification—he went to find his guru to fall in repentance at his feet. But Bṛhaspati, wanting to teach Indra a lesson, became invisible. Because Indra lost the blessings of Bṛhaspati, demonic forces were able to attack Indrapurī, wounding Indra and others.

The Need for a Spiritual Master

Like Indra, every human being needs the grace of a spiritual master. We may not face enemies like Indra's, but we still need protection as we pursue the business of human life: spiritual advancement. "Demons," such as our desires for material things, constantly seek our destruction.

Those of us who have taken to Kṛṣṇa consciousness want to attain a kingdom far superior to Indrapurī. We're aiming for the spiritual world, the kingdom of God, Kṛṣṇa. We know that the pleasure of serving Kṛṣṇa there is higher than anything Indra enjoys. Our plea for entrance into that service is the mantra Hare Kṛṣṇa, Hare Kṛṣṇa, Kṛṣṇa Kṛṣṇa, Hare Hare/ Hare Rāma, Hare Rāma, Rāma Rāma, Hare Hare.

We can know about chanting the holy names only when we've learned the purpose of life from a bona fide guru. Human beings are mostly at a loss to see the purpose in the gigantic creation around them. Using only observation and experience, people sometimes reason that an intelligent being created everything for some purpose. But the nature of the creator, the purpose of His creation, and the means to align with that purpose escapes them. These things must be revealed from beyond the creation, by the creator or His representatives. Therefore, to understand these things, everyone needs a guru. All gurus also have gurus, the ultimate guru being the Lord Himself. The principle of accepting personal guidance in the mission of life is so important that when Kṛṣṇa incarnates He also accepts a guru to set an example.

When we find a genuine guru who comes in a chain of teachers and disciples that starts with the Lord Himself, we learn that creation is meant to help fallen souls pursue material desires and ultimately return to their original spiritual position. A bona fide guru also teaches that the principal means of achieving the ultimate purpose of existence—loving union with Kṛṣṇa—is the chanting of His holy names, especially the *mahā-mantra:* Hare Kṛṣṇa, Hare Kṛṣṇa, Kṛṣṇa Kṛṣṇa, Hare Hare/ Hare Rāma, Hare Rāma, Rāma Rāma, Hare Hare.

When Kṛṣṇa incarnates He also accepts a guru to set an example.

Initiation and Spiritual Training

Even to know about the Lord's name requires some touch with a guru. So unquestionably someone who decides to dedicate his or her life to Kṛṣṇa will need systematic training by a guru. Just as a young couple formalize their relationship with marriage, or a student officially enrolls in a school, a person serious about loving and surrendering to Kṛṣṇa makes a vow of formal commitment. When we become officially initiated into a lineage of gurus and disciples, we receive a firm commitment to our deliverance from the guru who initiates us, the many previous teachers, and the Lord Himself. In ordinary life, when the admissions officer of a school accepts a student, all the teachers and staff, up to the chief administrator, give their implied assurance that they will do their utmost to ensure the student's education and graduation. Similarly, a faithful disciple in a transcendent school is sure to achieve spiritual success. At the time of initiation, the guru "plants the seed of devotion" and delivers the holy name by requesting Kṛṣṇa to manifest Himself through the chanting.

Kṛṣṇa will not manifest through the chanting if the chanter disrespects the guru—either the guru from whom one learned the chanting or the guru from whom one received formal initiation into the school of devotional life. Even in an ordinary school students who lack courtesy toward their teachers may be neglected or even dismissed. How much is the Lord displeased when someone disregards a spiritual master!

The offense to the holy name of disregarding or disobeying the guru stems from considering the guru an ordinary person. Of course, the guru almost always seems to be like us, appearing in a physical body made of the same ingredients as all other human beings. But the guru is the representative of God, is realized in the science of devotion, and is therefore extraordinary. Although police officers are human beings like you and I, we treat them with the respect due to the government as a whole because they represent the government and know the law. We respect a teacher as a representative of the school and a repository of knowledge and experience that exceeds our own. With such examples, we can easily understand that one should treat the guru, as we are taught, like God; the guru represents God and is our link to Him.

The scriptures list specific ways by which disciples must show respect for the guru. For example, they should sprinkle on their head water that has washed the guru's feet, and upon seeing the guru, they should offer prostrated obeisances. They shouldn't use the guru's bed, seat, shoes, or conveyances, worship anyone else as guru in the guru's presence, or act or speak in a way that displeases the guru.

One should worship the guru first and then take permission to worship Kṛṣṇa. Therefore, along with the picture or deity form of Kṛṣṇa, a disciple keeps a picture of his or her guru. The incense, flowers, and so forth, are offered first to the guru and then to Kṛṣṇa. Even when chanting the holy name of Kṛṣṇa, one keeps the guru in mind, with gratitude for the gift of chanting.

The disciple is expected to be not only respectful but also obedient. The guru's instructions—in both letter and spirit—should be the life and soul of the disciple. The guru often gives general and individual instructions. Some may apply to all times, places, and circumstances, such as the instruction to always remember Kṛṣṇa and never forget Him. Some are to be applied in various ways and degrees, depending on the situation. And not everything the guru says is an order; he may also give guidelines.

The disciple must avoid both neglect of the rules and blind, fanatical following. The key is to distinguish between eternal principles and external details. Kṛṣṇa therefore says that the disciple should inquire from the guru and follow the practical example of saints, or sadhus.

Beware of Cheaters

Some people today may feel that the scriptural rules for respecting one's guru are excessive. Yet respect for a person who represents and speaks for a greater power is a sign of civilization and culture. For example, modern social norms demand respect for one's employer, professor, or a district court judge.

Unfortunately, there will always be people seeking respect and prestige by claiming spiritual authority, just as there are criminals who dress as policemen and phony schools and businesses that cheat innocent people of their money. A prospective disciple should therefore determine if the guru is a disciple in a bona fide line of teachers and disciples, just as one examines the educational credentials of university professors. A guru's main qualification is knowledge of Kṛṣṇa—not simply theoretical knowledge, but realized knowledge demonstrated by a practical life of dedication to the Lord.

Generally, when one finds a bona fide guru, the relationship is established for eternity. Still, a guru is obliged to renounce a disciple who seriously or repeatedly falls from the path, and a disciple should reject a fallen guru.

From the Guru, One Gets Kṛṣṇa

If we please our spiritual master, then Kṛṣṇa in the form of His holy name will easily reveal Himself to us, even if we are not very qualified otherwise. This principle operates even in ordinary material dealings. For example, a highly placed university professor who feels that a certain student shows promise can recommend that student for an advanced program for which the student would not ordinarily be eligible. The institution will back up the professor's recommendation. Kṛṣṇa reciprocates in a similar way with His dear devotees. If Kṛṣṇa's representative is happy with our service, Kṛṣṇa accepts us despite our shortcomings. The obstacles to our chanting are then easily removed, and our progress is swift and sure.

CHAPTER 7

Receiving and Giving the Holy Name

The glory of the Lord's holy name is confidential and must be passed on to others with care.

Among the many presents I received for my sixth birthday were several pairs of heavy red stockings. Like most children, I preferred toys to clothes—especially duplicate clothes. So I ran to my room and pouted. Like any good mother, mine told me to return to my guests, smile, and say, "Thank you," regardless of how I felt about the gifts.

We commonly show what value we place on things by how we treat them. If I respect the gift or the giver, I place the object in a position of honor or give it to someone I care for. Giving what I have received to an unworthy person or throwing it carelessly into storage shows my lack of regard for it and may invoke the displeasure of the giver.

There's an example of this in the scriptures. While the sage Durvāsā was passing on the road, he saw Indra, chief celestial administrator, riding on the back of his elephant. Durvāsā was pleased to offer Indra a garland from his own neck. But proud Indra took the garland and, without respect

If we give a treasure to monkeys, the monkeys will respond only with attacking us, rather than with gratitude.

for Durvāsā Muni, placed it on the trunk of his elephant. Being an animal, the elephant couldn't understand the value of the garland and threw it between its legs and smashed it. Seeing this insulting behavior, Durvāsā cursed Indra to become poor. (*Śrīmad-Bhāgavatam* 8.5.15–16, Purport)

The fact that Indra was willing to part with a gift is laudatory. Giving in charity our possessions, whether earned or bestowed, is purifying even for saints. Indra's problem was that he gave in charity to an animal. Kṛṣṇa teaches in *Bhagavad-gītā* that charity should be given to a worthy person, at an appropriate time and place, without expecting return. If charity is given to someone who will misuse it, or if it is given disrespectfully, the giver becomes involved with the illusion of ignorance instead of advancing either materially or spiritually.

The greatest treasure is the holy name of the Lord, Kṛṣṇa. It is more precious than an alchemist's touchstone, which turns iron to gold. Our having received the holy name shows the love of those who gave it to us as well as our determination to know and love the Supreme Lord. To know of the glory, power, and love of the *mahā-mantra*—Hare Kṛṣṇa, Hare Kṛṣṇa, Kṛṣṇa Kṛṣṇa, Hare Hare/ Hare Rāma, Hare Rāma, Rāma Rāma, Hare Hare—is to know the essential intimate truth of all existence. Certainly when we have the fortune of the holy name we should also give it in charity.

Yet this treasure of Kṛṣṇa's name, which is identical to Kṛṣṇa, exhibits its full pleasure and peace only to one who honors it. One of the prime ways to show this honor is to use discretion when revealing the details of the name's glories. If we tell of the name's grandeur and sweetness to someone who then becomes blasphemous, we are also responsible for offending the holy name, and our spiritual advancement is impeded.

Jesus said, "Do not give what is holy to the dogs; nor cast your pearls before swine, lest they trample them under their feet, and turn and tear you in pieces." (Matthew 7:6) In a similar way, Kṛṣṇa tells Arjuna, "This confidential knowledge [of surrender to Kṛṣṇa with love] may never be explained to those who are not austere, or devoted, or engaged in devotional service, nor to one who is envious of Me." (*Bhagavad-gītā* 18.67)

Sharing the Name

Is the solution to keep spiritual knowledge to ourselves? No. For if out of fear of giving the holy name to swine-like envious people we refrain from sharing our spiritual wealth, we become envious as well. Śrīla Prabhupāda told one of his disciples, an expert cook, that to avoid envy she should teach her skills to others. An envious person wants to either take away what others have or prevent them from having access to his own opulence. Instead, we should want others to become as spiritually wealthy and fortunate as we are, or more so. In addition, by giving the charity of Kṛṣṇa consciousness to a worthy person, we evoke Kṛṣṇa's pleasure, thereby increasing our own happiness in chanting.

To share the holy name and the astonishing brilliance of Lord Kṛṣṇa's form, qualities, and activities with faithful, honest persons brings great joy and satisfaction. The reciprocation of wisdom and elation both between the people who exchange understanding and between them and Kṛṣṇa is so thrilling as to be almost indescribable. Kṛṣṇa says, "For one who explains the supreme secret to the devotees, pure devotional service is guaranteed, and at the end he will come back to Me. There is no servant in this world more dear to Me than he, nor will there ever be one more dear." (*Bhagavad-gītā* 18.68–69)

How to discern where and with whom to share the name? The Lord Himself in His incarnation as Caitanya Mahāprabhu would chant on the public streets with His devotees, leaving it up to the hearers to take advantage or not. But He was cautious about discussing intimate details of spiritual life with those who would be critical. Before we share more than the sound of the holy name with someone, we should try to find at least a spark of faith, for faith is the only real qualification for taking up the chanting of Kṛṣṇa's name.

For several years, a group of devotees of Kṛṣṇa traveled around America with two *sannyāsīs*—Viṣṇujana Swami and Tamāl Kṛṣṇa Goswami. Viṣṇujana Swami would sweetly sing the Hare Kṛṣṇa *mahā-mantra* while devotees would give out free plates of *prasādam.* Tamāl Kṛṣṇa Goswami told his friend Ravīndra Svarūpa Dāsa that he would walk up to those who were eating and listening and ask, "Do you like the food and the music?" If they showed some enthusiasm, he would introduce them to Prabhupāda's books or discuss philosophy with them. If they had little or no attraction to the chanting or the meal, he spent no further time with them.

In other words, the faith of people will show in their eagerness. Jesus speaks again of the Lord's glory in terms of a pearl: "The kingdom of God is like a merchant in search of fine pearls; on finding one pearl of great value, he went and sold all that he had and bought it." (Matthew 13:45–46) Rūpa Gosvāmī similarly explains, "Pure devotional service in Kṛṣṇa consciousness can be attained only by paying one price—

Faith is the only real qualification for taking up the chanting of Kṛṣṇa's name.

---

that is, intense greed to obtain it. If it is available somewhere, one must purchase it without delay." (*Padyāvalī* 14)

Proper Discretion

But practicing discretion in sharing the truth is more than a blanket categorization of two kinds of people—faithful and faithless. The reality is that there are few people with whom one can share either everything or nothing. The key to avoiding the offense of teaching the faithless, while at the same time benefiting ourselves and others, is to develop fine judgment regarding appropriateness. Lord Kṛṣṇa gives four guidelines for spiritual communication: the message must be true, pleasing, backed by scriptural authority, and beneficial to both parties. For a specific message to be beneficial, one needs to determine its appropriateness. For example, many truths of spiritual life seem bitter to someone with material attachments. Transcendent realization involves not only the wonderful and exciting revelation of Kṛṣṇa's name, form, and activities, but also the fact that in our separation from Kṛṣṇa we are voluntarily in an illusion of selfish, greedy ugliness. To progress in understanding our eternal nature, we must face the unpleasant truth that trying to enjoy a temporary, miserable material body and mind is at best a great embarrassment for us, the soul.

Although an understanding of the awkward situation of a soul in the world is undoubtedly ultimately beneficial for everyone, there should be a type of contract before such instruction is given. Otherwise, if the intended recipient becomes angry there is no benefit, and there may be harm, for him or her as well as for the giver of the message, Therefore, Prabhupāda says, "One should not speak in such a way as to agitate the minds of others. Of course, when a teacher speaks, he can speak the truth for the instruction of his students, but such a teacher should not speak to those who are not his students if he will agitate their minds." In other words, however true our instruction, a person should formally or informally accept us in the role of teacher for it to have true benefit. Of course, being pleasing is also important. Our presentation should be civilized and polished.

The principle that our hearers must in some regard be our students before we can speak bitter truth or advanced topics holds true even when we share Kṛṣṇa consciousness with faithful people. For example, readers of this book have agreed to hear something from me. When someone gives a public lecture, the audience takes at least the temporary position of students. The same is true when people take the initiative to ask for advice: they are to some extent approaching us as an authority, giving us the right to say something that will benefit them, even if sometimes unpleasant. Without such a contract, whether formal or understood, we're not justified in communicating whatever we want in the name of truth. To do so on spiritual topics is to offend the name, and if done with a devotee of Kṛṣṇa, may be an offense to the Lord's servant as well.

In his book *Harināma Cintamāṇi,* Bhaktivinoda Ṭhākura especially explains the offense of teaching the holy name to the faithless in regard to those who act as gurus. Whether initiating disciples into the chanting, or having a formal relationship as an instructing spiritual master, there is sometimes a temptation to accept disciples for personal wealth or prestige. Such a problem occurs in ordinary schools. Universities sometimes admit students not solely because of their academic qualifications, but because they come from families that will give generously of their money, name, or both. It's no secret that the most selective universities give preference to such "legacy students." They openly say that favoring the legacy candidate saves other students' tuition costs because of the donations received.

Perhaps such a policy makes financial and practical sense to a school of engineering or law, but it runs counter to Kṛṣṇa's desire and the whole mood of devotional service to Him. A guru can suffer if he considers a disciple's qualification in terms other than faith.

Sometimes, of course, we imperfect beings may be deceived by the apparent sincerity of someone who shows interest in Kṛṣṇa's service. A merciful devotee of Kṛṣṇa wants to give a chance to everyone, fanning even a small spark of curiosity into a blaze of loving devotion. If by accident we take as a student or disciple someone who later becomes blasphemous, we should publicly renounce that person so that both of us do not fall from the Lord's shelter.

If we wish our chanting of Hare Kṛṣṇa, Hare Kṛṣṇa, Kṛṣṇa Kṛṣṇa, Hare Hare/ Hare Rāma, Hare Rāma, Rāma Rāma, Hare Hare to have the full effect, we must treat the holy name and all transcendent knowledge and practice with love and care. We honor the Absolute Truth through scrupulously giving the blasphemous little opportunity to find fault, teaching only what will benefit faithful persons who agree to hear from us, and finding great satisfaction and bliss always sharing the holy name with those eager to enter its mysteries.

CHAPTER 8

Esteem for Sacred Writings

Pure chanting of God's names requires reverence for God in all His forms, including scripture.

It is fashionable in modern secular societies to regard sacred literature as the mythological musings of undeveloped people. Schools teach that with our current understanding of physics, medicine, psychology, democracy, and so on, we have little use for such writings except as literary art. Those who take scripture literally are pegged with pejorative terms such as "fundamentalists." It may be stylish to borrow ideas from the Vedic scriptures—yoga, meditation, mantra chanting. But living by the laws of scripture is seen as outmoded and simplistic.

To get the spiritual benefit of chanting Kṛṣṇa's names, however, requires a reverence for Kṛṣṇa in all His forms, including His scriptures. Kṛṣṇa appeared on earth in His original form about five thousand years ago. After He departed to His eternal abode, His "literary incarnation," Vyāsadeva, compiled the cream of Vedic scripture, *Śrīmad-Bhāgavatam.* Śrīla Prabhupāda wrote that reading this scripture is identical to seeing Kṛṣṇa in person. Because the words of the *Bhāgavatam* describe Kṛṣṇa, they are spiritually identical to Him. If we blaspheme the *Bhāgavatam,* other Vedic books, or literature in pursuance of the Vedic version, we offend the holy name, greatly impeding our progress in chanting.

What do we mean by "Vedic literature"? Unlike modern scholars, Śrīla Prabhupāda did not use the term *Vedic* to denote only a particular period in the history of India. Following the previous spiritual masters in his line, he justifiably used the term to apply to all the traditional sacred books of India. And "literature in pursuance of the Vedic version" refers to any books that, like the *Vedas,* direct us toward a proper understanding of our relationship with God.

We avoid this offense against Kṛṣṇa's holy name if we accept the concept of scripture in general, revere authentic scriptures of traditions other than our own, respect but avoid scriptures that teach valid yet lesser religious practice, and reject pseudo scripture that opposes love of God.

We also avoid this offense by worshiping Kṛṣṇa with our intelligence through careful study and application of sacred literature. Such study infuses us with both eagerness and direction for attaining devotional service to the Lord. We take our happiness from exploring each aspect of the Vedic scriptures we read. And we scrupulously adhere to the obvious meanings and applications consistent with both the texts as a whole and the examples of liberated souls.

A Culture of Enlightenment

One reason people reject the very concept of sacred writing is that the word *scripture* to them conjures up the ghosts of societies that forbade smiling on the Sabbath, or declared that the way to perfection was a system of intricate ritualistic procedures that few could perform and even fewer understand. Besides, scriptures contain fantastic stories of miracles and supernatural happenings that modern science claims it discredited long ago. And aren't scriptures the product of imperfect persons?

The reality is that when correctly understood and applied, genuine scripture acts like a guidebook and instruction manual for human life and the cosmos. It is the procedure brochure for the enterprise of the material creation. From scripture, coupled with oral tradition, we learn of methods of spiritual elevation, including the chanting of the holy name. From scripture we learn of the lives of past saints, sages, and incarnations of Kṛṣṇa. In fact, the stories of scripture, whether in written or oral form, are the basis for the transmission and foundation of a culture of enlightenment.

Making Sense of the Fantastic

Certainly it is true that many stories in sacred writings seem fantastic to our scientific world. But many current technological wonders seemed fictional and implausible only a few decades ago. It is not, therefore, implausible that former societies could have had abilities and expertise unavailable today. For example, ancient architecture in Peru is virtually impossible to re-create using modern methods. The view that technology has always progressed and could never have been greater than it is today may be inaccurate. Indeed, even recent history indicates that much knowledge existed in ancient Greece, was lost to Europe in the Middle Ages, and then gradually resurfaced. It is reasonable and logical, then, to assume that what is commonplace today, such as television and the Internet, may be lost and forgotten in the future, only to resurface later.

Additionally, even today there is much strong empirical evidence for the existence of the supernatural. But because current science can't explain the evidence, it is usually suppressed. Also, the *Vedas*—with their information about spirit and subtle matter—provide a world view that makes the seemingly impossible easy to accept. For example, once you understand that spirit, or life, is independent of matter, it's easy to believe that living beings can live anywhere in the universe and do all kinds of amazing things.

A valid complaint about scripture for the spiritually minded is that much of it focuses on ritual and material gain. Kṛṣṇa validates that sentiment when He tells His friend Arjuna that those who have practiced yoga in previous lives are above most scriptural rituals. The sad truth, however, is that few people are interested in genuine spiritual realization. Therefore, Kṛṣṇa and His great devotees give instructions and examples in scripture for all types of people. There are different scriptures for various classes of people with diverse inclinations and desires. And there may be various levels and kinds of instruction in the same scriptural canon.

Sometimes the Lord, His agent, or His son may teach eternal truths at a lower level or in an obscured way according to time, place, or circumstance. Scriptures that arise from such teachings may teach less than pure, unmotivated devotion to the Lord, but they serve the function of gradually bringing people to the pinnacle of realization. Knowing that perfection is generally achieved over many lifetimes, one absorbed in chanting the mantra of the ultimate truth supports and encourages those at various levels.

Bona fide scripture, by definition, comes directly from God or from souls liberated from the imperfections and cheating of common persons. The unadulterated truth can flow through a person free from selfish desires and linked with God, just as the view of the world outside can pass through a clear window.

Kṛṣṇa reveals Himself in the pages of scripture when we study with rapt attention.

A Role for Discrimination

Still, one shouldn't accept simply any writing as sacred just because it claims to be so. Part of the offense of blaspheming scripture is to accept a philosophy contrary to serving the personal form of the Lord with devotion. Also, if a "religious" system claims that other genuine methods and scriptures are sinful, it should be abandoned as small-minded sectarianism. In addition, we should reject any system or philosophy that denies the soul, the Personality of Godhead, the process of developing love for God, or the goal of individual loving union with Him. Therefore, chanting Hare Kṛṣṇa while holding a monistic attitude—thinking that the ultimate reality is simply energy and light—is part of this offense to the holy name.

A devotee of Lord Kṛṣṇa should depend only on traditions that expound *bhakti*—loving devotion to the person Kṛṣṇa. Offering respect from a distance, one should avoid scripture that promotes yogic powers, good works for heavenly rewards, or salvation devoid of *bhakti,* what to speak of lower forms of worship aimed at power gained through propitiating ghostly or demonic beings.

Śrīla Bhaktivinoda Ṭhākura's *Harināma Cintāmaṇi* lists nine essential principles of *kṛṣṇa-bhakti.* We can identify *bhakti* scriptures as those that promote these nine principles: (1) There is one Supreme Lord, Kṛṣṇa. (2) He is the possessor of all energies. (3) Kṛṣṇa is the fountainhead of transcendental relationships and is situated in His own spiritual world, where He eternally gives joy to all living beings. (4) Living beings are particles of the Lord, unlimited in number, infinitesimal in size, and conscious. (5) Some living beings have been bound in material universes from time beyond memory, attracted by illusory pleasure. (6) Some living beings are eternally liberated and engaged in worshiping

Kṛṣṇa; they reside with Him as associates in the spiritual sky and experience love for Him. (7) Kṛṣṇa exists with His energies—material, spiritual, and the living beings—in a state of simultaneous identity and differentiation, permeating all yet remaining aloof. (8) The process for the living being to realize Kṛṣṇa is nine-fold: hearing about Kṛṣṇa, chanting, remembering, serving, worshiping, praying, acting as His servant, being His friend, and surrendering everything. (9) The ultimate goal of a living being is pure love for Kṛṣṇa, which Kṛṣṇa awakens in a soul out of His mercy.

If one follows the most pure scriptures, rejects assorted worldly traditions masquerading as sacred, and respects genuine scripture that's at a lower level, there still must be care in scriptural study. Even an eternal tradition of untainted written or oral revelation can become skewed through imaginative interpretation and usage. To respect scripture, we understand it using the most clear and direct meaning possible, studying the practical precedents of past and present pure devotees of Kṛṣṇa. We also approach scripture through the direction of a guru, who gives specific guidance for what is relevant to our present circumstance. Misinterpretation or misapplication of scripture can be more dangerous than denying it altogether. A wolf disguised as a sheep is far more dangerous than an obvious wolf.

With so many considerations and confusions about scripture, wouldn't it be better to simply chant Hare Kṛṣṇa, Hare Kṛṣṇa, Kṛṣṇa Kṛṣṇa, Hare Hare/ Hare Rāma, Hare Rāma, Rāma Rāma, Hare Hare, and forget scripture completely? It is true that chanting alone can bring us to perfection. But it must be offenseless chanting, which requires a reverential attitude toward genuine sacred writings.

Oh, but how much pleasure and solace there is in scripture! We can gain much joy and confidence from reading the

Bhagavad-gītā, the words of Kṛṣṇa Himself. And we can find similar succor in works of contemporary writers—devotees who take the principles Kṛṣṇa elucidated and apply them to familiar situations.

Of course, relish and delight are not our only motives for reading sacred writings. We *need* scripture. To ascertain truth without scripture, we have little choice but to rely on our own sensual and mental faculties and those of others. These alone can give us only partial, relative knowledge. Our senses are imperfect, even when enhanced with sophisticated instruments. We make mistakes from habit, carelessness, or unconscious bias. We tend to cheat—even to cheat ourselves. And when we identify the body as the self, we are living in a general illusion. Therefore, axiomatic truths—the starting point for logical and sensory conclusions—must come from a source free of defects if we want to base our actions on perfect knowledge.

When our foundational knowledge comes from the Absolute Truth, then chanting Kṛṣṇa's holy name will quickly propel us on the path to Him. Hearing from scripture about the beauty of Kṛṣṇa's form and the superb activities of the spiritual world will inspire us to chant with intense desire for His loving service. Pleased with our desire, Kṛṣṇa will cleanse us with a downpour of His mercy, and our progress will be swift indeed.

CHAPTER 9

The Mood of Surrender

Success in chanting the Lord's holy names requires both faith and a willingness to let go of harmful material attachments.

A real summer job—not babysitting! I made it to the hotel before six in the morning so as to have the breakfast buns done on time. Sweating in front of a wall of ovens, we turned out cakes, pies, and bread. All of us in the kitchen were servants of the hotel. We had to cook what was on the menu, following our given recipes and rules. But I was unlike the others in at least one respect: Most of them felt that their job was simply a step to becoming a hotel manager themselves. While they labored as servants, their hearts yearned to become the masters.

The ambition to be the master is certainly the stuff of worldly success. But spiritual achievement requires the opposite: the more one is a servant, the higher one's position. Accustomed through habits of many lifetimes, we conditioned souls assume that happiness, knowledge, and vitality will come by grasping and controlling the world. But these actually come from letting go of our false ego as controllers and enjoyers and, instead, holding on to the feet of the Lord, Śrī Kṛṣṇa, as His servants.

Imagine that we see in front of us what appears to be all we desire. But when we reach out to grab those pleasures, we find instead a solid block to our progress. Turning around, we find the source of real enjoyment. Pleasure from trying to exploit life and matter appears in front of us, but it is only a reflection, as in a mirror. There is no substance to that satisfaction. The mirror is catching the image, in a twisted way, of what fallen souls have turned their back to—service to God. Accessing that service and concomitant pleasure, however, requires us to often do exactly the opposite of what seems to bring fulfillment in this world.

Our habit of embracing materialistic, self-centered plans and solutions is long standing. Anyone starting on the spiritual path is expected to be full of such mundane attachments, with merely a spark of interest in surrender to Kṛṣṇa, though that ember may seem significant to a beginner. As we progress in a life of holy service, we gradually become aware of our foolish attempts to enjoy a reflection. Such awareness comes to our consciousness primarily through the grace of Śrī Kṛṣṇa, who from within our hearts reveals the truth about Himself and the dirt remaining within us. Kṛṣṇa's revelation is a response to any and all service we do for Him with devotion. Our primary means of serving and evoking His pleasure is through the chanting of His holy name, as in the *mahā-mantra:* Hare Kṛṣṇa, Hare Kṛṣṇa, Kṛṣṇa Kṛṣṇa, Hare Hare/ Hare Rāma, Hare Rāma, Rāma Rāma, Hare Hare.

As we are chanting, however, if we consciously and deliberately maintain our illusory position as master of the world, we try to accomplish two irreconcilable purposes, and thus cheat the holy name. Our chanting is then only official, as if some shallow ritual, and Kṛṣṇa in the form of His name is offended. We become like the hotel dishwasher who, while seemingly revering his boss, is enviously desiring his position.

The material world is a reflection of the spiritual, and, like any reflection, cannot give real satisfaction, although it may appear to contain pleasurable objects

Lack of Faith

Generally, this offense to the holy name comes from a lack of faith. We know that material life over-promises and under-delivers, yet we fear that holding the diamond of devotion will mean letting go of our broken bits of colored glass, carefully gathered on the shores of our many lives. We fear that the diamond is false and that the glass, once abandoned, cannot be reclaimed.

The scriptures describe this offense as "not having complete faith in the holy name and maintaining material attachments even after understanding so many instructions on this matter." The very fact that the scripture tells us that we many be holding on to material attachments while chanting Hare Kṛṣṇa is instructive. In the *Bhagavad-gītā* Kṛṣṇa states that He destroys the ignorance in the heart of a person absorbed in His glories. In the *Bhāgavatam* we learn that hearing Kṛṣṇa's name and activities eradicates our materialistic consciousness. Based on scriptural quotes such as these, some people claim purification of material attachment to be automatic for anyone chanting the holy name. But if the cleaning of our heart happens with no effort on our part, how would it be possible to "maintain material attachments" while chanting?

Kṛṣṇa does not interfere with the living being's free will. Our ability to desire is the defining principle of being alive. Though Descartes claimed that thinking is the prime indicator of existence, more primal than thinking is feeling, desire. Kṛṣṇa will illumine our heart, showing us what is valuable and what is trash. We then have to want Kṛṣṇa to remove the garbage. If we persist in holding on to our lust, envy, greed, illusion and so forth, after Kṛṣṇa reveals these to us, He won't change us against our will. We'll keep our rubbish—and offend the Lord. By chanting we invite Kṛṣṇa to purify us, to make us fit for His service and entrance into the spiritual world. If after inviting Him we refuse to follow His direction, how will He be pleased?

We can understand this principle through an everyday example. Sometimes a friend might invite us to help clean up a storage area. As we go through their belongings, if they want to keep everything—no matter how old, broken, or unused—then we would ask, "Why did you ask me to come?"

To avoid this block to our progress, we need to nurture a mood of surrender while we chant and live a life of such surrender moment by moment.

Unworthy Shelters

Here we'll examine some specific symptoms of the materialistic mentality we need to avoid, and then consider the six facets of surrender.

Materialists feel sheltered and empowered by their insatiable desire for mental and physical pleasure. Greed, lust, anger, and arrogance seem like friends and protectors who will give both impetus for the drive to success and armor against attacks along the way. Obstacles or reversals, including people who oppose one's plans, need to be dispensed with through one's own intelligence and power. People think they will achieve happiness, knowledge, and security by manipulating their environment.

People may think they will achieve fulfillment by getting everything to behave as they like—nature, other people, their own body and mind, anyone and anything. Kṛṣṇa calls such thinking demonic, directly opposed to saintly character. The irony is that this mentality can disguise itself as *bhakti,* loving service to Kṛṣṇa. How? We may feel that other devotees of Kṛṣṇa need to change their behavior to support our own service to Kṛṣṇa, or that our pleasure in such service depends on our control of our environment. While in a spiritual process, we may keep trying to control and change the outer world to get satisfaction. Kṛṣṇa therefore states that those opposed to Him consider the lust of material desire to be their shelter and protector.

Six Aspects of Spiritual Surrender

In contrast, *mahātmās,* or great souls, find their shelter in Kṛṣṇa's spiritual energy. This energy is the Lord's most exalted devotee, Śrīmatī Rādhārāṇī. Unlike the witch of misleading lust, Rādhārāṇī is the soothing mother of love, presenting us to Kṛṣṇa, the supreme father. Coming under her protection involves six aspects that directly counteract and contradict the materialistic tendencies that have only brought us despair and disappointment.

First, we should accept anything favorable for Kṛṣṇa's service, and use in a favorable way situations we cannot change. We do not need to guess what is helpful for serving the Lord. The scriptures, gurus, and saintly persons give clear instructions in this regard. For example, we are advised to take a firm vow to chant the Hare Kṛṣṇa *mahā-mantra* a minimum number of times daily. Further, we should wake up before sunrise, using the early morning for chanting, worship, and scriptural study. Having such a program follows the example of great devotees.

Our vegetarian meals should be offered first to Kṛṣṇa, considering Him the master of our house, who must eat before we, His servants, partake of our meals. We should see our duties as having been given to us by Kṛṣṇa and use the fruits of our activities for His pleasure. Our time should be spent in devotional service. Confident of achieving the perfection of life through our service to Kṛṣṇa, we should continue with patience and enthusiasm in both the ups and downs of the waves of the material modes.

Sometimes seemingly unfavorable situations come unbidden and beyond our ability to alter. We may become sick or injured and unable to externally perform our worship of Kṛṣṇa. Others may insult us or treat us unfairly, unsettling our mind. The weather may prevent our planned trip to the temple. While the demonic tendency is to try to eliminate all such obstacles though manipulating externals, one who wants spiritual success seeks to understand the Lord's purpose.

A good teacher gives lessons and homework that highlight students' weaknesses. To complete the assignment and pass the exam, a student must understand and apply what was lacking. Similarly, Kṛṣṇa will set up situations we can use for spiritual advantage if we address and correct some area of weakness or lack within ourselves. Such apparently unfavorable situations, therefore, when understood and used properly, are truly the great favor of Kṛṣṇa.

Second, we have to reject anything irredeemably unfavorable for Kṛṣṇa's devotional service. Activities that must be absolutely discarded are gambling, illicit sex (sex should be in marriage for procreation), taking intoxicants, and eating meat, fish or eggs. Furthermore, it is best to work for only as much money, knowledge, and achievement as will help us think of Kṛṣṇa with love and spread His glories. We should give up friends, objects, activities, and discussions that drag our heart from the Lord, or deal with them only superficially. If we live simply, preferably in a society of Kṛṣṇa's devotees, avoiding problems is much easier.

Third, humility, or the lack of desire to receive the honor of others, is an essential requirement for receiving the enlightenment that will erase even difficult attachments.

True humility is gratitude for Kṛṣṇa's gifts, joy at the privilege of service to Him, and an honest appraisal of our position in the universe.

Fourth, a surrendered soul looks only to Kṛṣṇa for protection. While we certainly have a duty to live a healthy life and take normal measures to protect ourselves (seatbelts, for example), ultimately the protection of our body, mind, and advancement in Kṛṣṇa's service is in Kṛṣṇa's hands. Acknowledging Kṛṣṇa as the controller gives us a deep sense of inner peace no matter how great the present difficulty.

Fifth, we should depend exclusively on the mercy of Kṛṣṇa for our maintenance. We should not claim to be able to maintain ourselves independently. And when taking help from others, we must know that ultimately Kṛṣṇa is working through them. Everything that comes to us does so by His sanction only.

The sixth facet of surrender is to have no interest other than Kṛṣṇa's interest. That implies harmony, not the absence of personal initiative. Just as all family members can work for the good of the family by their individual plans and desires, so one can interlock personal plans and aspirations with Kṛṣṇa's will. A surrendered devotee understands Kṛṣṇa to be the whole and knows that by pleasing Kṛṣṇa we please ourselves when we're connected to Him with love.

For most people, chanting Kṛṣṇa's holy names with faith and without material attachments is a gradual process. Most of us start on the spiritual path with many material desires. The chanting itself is the key to attaining a holy inner and outer life. As we chant, we see things more clearly, from the spiritual perspective. If we use that clarity to improve the spiritual quality of our lives, we will attain the full potency of chanting, which will quickly bring us to the fulfillment of our true desire: union of love with Kṛṣṇa.

CHAPTER 10

Whose Name Is God's Name?

God has innumerable names, but does that mean that all names are God's?

This chapter deals with what is listed in the *Padma Purāṇa* (*Brahmā Khaṇḍa 25.16*) as the second offense in chanting the holy names:

śivasya śrī-viṣṇor ya iha
guṇa-nāmādi-sakalaṁ
dhiyā bhinnaṁ paśyet sa khalu
hari-nāmāhita-karaḥ

Devotees in ISKCON are familiar with this translation by Śrila Prabhupāda: "To consider the names of demigods like Lord Śiva or Lord Brahmā to be equal to, or independent of, the name of Lord Viṣṇu." Prabhupāda elaborates on the meaning of the verse in various places. To aid our understanding of those explanations, here is a word-by-word translation of the verse:

śivasya—the name of Lord Śiva; *śrī-viṣṇor*—Lord Viṣṇu; *yaḥ*—who; *iha*—in this material world; *guṇa*—qualities;

nāma—name; *ādi-sakalam*—everything; *dhiyā*—with the conception; *bhinnam*—difference; *paśyet*—may see; *saḥ*—he; *khalu*—indeed; *hari-nāmā*—the holy name of the Lord; *ahita-karaḥ*—inauspicious or blasphemous

I'll discuss four lessons drawn from this verse that can help us avoid this particular offense in chanting the Lord's names. The first lesson is that all names of God are equally holy. The second is that while all names of God are identical with Him, they reveal a variety of moods of interaction with Him. The third is that names that refer to beings other than God, even demigods (*devas*), are not equal to names of God. And the fourth is to understand the relationship between Śiva and Kṛṣṇa.

All Names of God Are Equally Holy

Śrīla Prabhupāda writes: "The second offense is to see the holy names of the Lord in terms of worldly distinction. The Lord is the proprietor of all the universes, and therefore He may be known in different places by different names, but that does not in any way qualify the fullness of the Lord. Any nomenclature which is meant for the Supreme Lord is as holy as the others because they are all meant for the Lord. Such holy names are as powerful as the Lord, and there is no bar for anyone in any part of the creation to chant and glorify the Lord by the particular name of the Lord as it is locally understood. They are all auspicious, and one should not distinguish such names of the Lord as material commodities." (*Śrīmad-Bhāgavatam* 2.1.11, Purport)

Much suffering, even up to the point of torture and war, takes place because of wrangling over the nomenclature of the Supreme Lord. If you don't like my name for God, you might call me a heretic. But it's reasonable that God, who creates and owns everything, has innumerable names. Even we ordinary people have many names, such as legal names, pet names, nicknames, and titles. Sometimes what appear to be various names for God are only the same term in different languages, including names that mean things like "the Provider," "the Sustainer," "the Healer," or "the Creator." Followers of the Vedic scriptures have long sung the thousand names of Viṣṇu in the Sanskrit tongue, and other religious systems teach ninety-nine names, fifteen names, and so forth, according to their language and understanding.

If a devotee of God who calls on any one of His holy names perceives the other names of God in terms of worldly distinctions, the name is offended—because God is fully present in His name. He turns away from such narrow-minded self-righteousness.

Kṛṣṇa's Name Is Kṛṣṇa Himself, Full of Spiritual Variety

"In this material world," Śrīla Prabhupāda writes, "the holy name of Viṣṇu is all-auspicious. Viṣṇu's name, form, qualities, and pastimes are all transcendental, absolute knowledge. Therefore, if one tries to separate the Absolute Personality of Godhead from His holy name or His transcendental form, qualities, and pastimes, thinking them to be material, that is offensive.... This is the second offense at the lotus feet of the holy name of the Lord." (*Caitanya-caritāmṛta, Ādi-līlā* 8.24, Purport)

First we learned to respect equally all names of God. Now we learn to respect Kṛṣṇa's name as being absolutely the same as Himself. There is no mundane hierarchy in the different names of God. God is one, and His names are also one. There are not many gods. Yet, as the Lord Himself has various incarnations and expansions, His innumerable names also display different moods or flavors of spirituality. For example, some names of Kṛṣṇa are more intimate than others, just as "sweetheart" is a more intimate form of address than "Your Honor"—even though they may refer to the same person.

Names like "the Creator," "the Sustainer," and so on, relate to God's role in the material creation or in our lives here. Like "judge" and "Your Honor," they tell us something of God "at work." Focusing on Kṛṣṇa's dealings with *our* concerns, these names tend to be human-centered.

Other names of God concern His pastimes in His spiritual abode. While these names may also indicate Kṛṣṇa's dealings with others, those "others" are His pure devotees, not rebellious souls.

Unfortunately, most of the world's genuine spiritual and religious traditions know only of God's names in relation to the material creation. There is little knowledge of Kṛṣṇa's personal life in His own kingdom, or of His names there. When this knowledge exists, it is generally not part of the mainstream religious teaching or practice. In contrast, the Vaiṣṇava schools, and particularly Gauḍīya Vaiṣṇavism (including the Hare Kṛṣṇa movement), provide all members with rich, detailed information about Kṛṣṇa's divine realm, devotees, activities, and names.

Śrīla Prabhupāda explains that the name *Kṛṣṇa* is the supreme name because it means "all attractive." It includes all aspects of the Lord and encompasses God's qualities of both opulence and sweetness. Because Kṛṣṇa is the original Personality of Godhead, all other names of God are included within His name.

Kṛṣṇa's devotees distribute His name because they wish to envelop others in the divine sweetness that surpasses immersion in the Lord's opulence and majesty. Names that express God's functions in this world give less than

The sweetness of Kṛṣṇa's names related to His Vṛndāvana devotees and pastimes are like honey, surpassing even the majestic opulence of Vaikuṇṭha.

the overflowing satisfaction for which the soul yearns. And the self-satisfied Lord feels much greater pleasure when addressed in relation to His dear saintly devotees than with names that glorify His role in the world.

Just as one who knows only the actions and names of God in relation to the material world should not reject the other names, so those who have the fortune of accessing Kṛṣṇa's intimate names should not think that superior knowledge makes the knower superior. Rather, with humility and equal vision those who chant and sing mantras such as Hare Kṛṣṇa, Hare Kṛṣṇa, Kṛṣṇa Kṛṣṇa, Hare Hare/ Hare Rāma, Hare Rāma, Rāma Rāma, Hare Hare should give all respect to persons absorbed only in a secondary understanding. Thus we will please the holy name.

Even within the kingdom of God there are varieties in the intensity of intimacy with Kṛṣṇa. But these varieties are not like "higher" and "lower" in the material world. One who thinks that a particular name is inferior because it is associated with the Lord's less intimate activities makes a worldly distinction about the name. And if one denigrates a devotee of God's regal forms and names, one compounds the offense.

Judging whether a particular name of God is seeped in awe or intimate love is not so simple anyway. Distinctions between the reverential, intimate, or most intimate names of God can rest more on the mood and understanding of those who call on the name than on a literal definition. Even Kṛṣṇa's most intimate devotees, His cowherd girlfriends, sometimes call Him Acutya (Infallible), Ṛṣabha (Greatest Person), or Nātha (Lord).

The distinctions between God's various forms and their corresponding names are not about potency but about relationship. Therefore, to nourish particular relationships, some forms and names of full expansions of Kṛṣṇa never display certain qualities of His. Each type of relationship with the Lord is glorious. When Kṛṣṇa descended as His own devotee, as Caitanya Mahāprabhu, He encouraged everyone to focus on God in His original form of complete sweetness and all relationships (Kṛṣṇa). But when He met persons purely devoted to Kṛṣṇa's forms such as Rāmacandra or Nārāyaṇa, He praised their attachment and love for God.

While God's descriptive names are innumerable, He doesn't "have" a name in the sense of owning an appellation that is arbitrary, temporary, and different from Him. A conditioned soul is different from the mind, body, and name. Therefore, when I call my friend's name, look at her picture, or think of her qualities, I don't have direct contact with her. But Kṛṣṇa, being absolute, is identical to His form, name, and qualities. Contact with any of them is direct contact with Him. While there is a simultaneous oneness and difference between the Lord and His energies, there is only oneness with His personal features, such as His name. To say and hear Kṛṣṇa's name with pure love is to be fully in His presence. This oneness of God and His name is true for all of His names, whether in relation to the creation or to the spiritual realm.

Kṛṣṇa's Names and Names of Beings Such As Demigods

Śrīla Prabhupāda writes, "To consider the names of demigods like Lord Śiva or Lord Brahmā to be equal to, or independent of, the name of Lord Viṣṇu.... If someone thinks that he can chant 'Kālī, Kālī!' or 'Durgā, Durgā!' and it is the same as Hare Kṛṣṇa, that is the greatest offense." (*The Nectar of Devotion,* Chapter 8)

A third lesson in avoiding this offense deals with the distinction between names of God and names of others. When we respect all names of Kṛṣṇa, we need to remember that not every name refers to Him. For example, many names of the Supreme Lord, such as "the Witness," could easily refer to someone other than God. In a court there are so many ordinary human beings who can be called "the witness." If we think, therefore, that any witness is God, we offend the name.

Similarly, some powerful beings, though God's servants, have names that can also refer to Him. Although Kṛṣṇa in His omnipotence and omnipresence can control and maintain everything Himself, out of love He engages highly realized or pure souls in His service. The Sanskrit terms for these beings are *devas* or *suras.* The English word Prabhupāda used to refer to this class of being is "demigods." They are living beings, souls like you and I and, indeed, all forms of life. Having chosen to live in goodness and purity, these souls have received bodies far more subtle, beautiful, and powerful than our earthly forms. Any soul has the potential to transmigrate into a *deva* form, or to fall from *deva* life into the human form or lower.

The chief *devas* have both titles and personal names. For example, the title of the leading administrative *deva* is "Indra," which means "chief." The current Indra is named Purandara. Sometimes a name or title can refer to either a *deva* or Kṛṣṇa. In the last mantra of the *Īśopaniṣad,* one of 108 scriptures dedicated to transcendental knowledge, the Supreme Lord is called Agni, which is also the title of the *deva* of fire. When referring to God, Agni means one who is as powerful as fire or is the source of fire. That Kṛṣṇa can be called Agni does not mean we can regard or worship the fire-god Agni as supreme.

Sometimes, in the name of following the Vedic scriptures, people worship *devas,* especially Śiva, Durgā, and Gaṇeśa, as if they were full incarnations of Kṛṣṇa. As described previously, Kṛṣṇa does not reveal Himself fully in all His incarnations and expansions. It may be confusing, therefore, to learn that Rāma is the Personality of Godhead but that Gaṇeśa, for example, is not.

How to know who is God and who is a *deva*? When does a name such as *Agni* or *Sūrya* refer to a *deva* and when to God? When is someone calling on the same God by a different name, and when is someone calling to something other than God? To answer these questions in specific instances, one has to refer to the scriptures under a bona fide guru's guidance, following the examples of saintly persons.

The *devas* are Kṛṣṇa's devotees in various degrees of realization and aspiration. Like any living being in the material world, their names are temporary designations, different from themselves. We automatically worship and please them when we chant Kṛṣṇa's name and worship Him, just as we satisfy our obligations to all government departments when we pay taxes to the central agency. If we approach the *devas* directly—which is not generally necessary or even recommended—it should be only to respect them as God's agents or to ask their assistance in our service to Him. The best way to worship *devas* is with food or articles first offered to Kṛṣṇa. While we should respect scriptures and traditions that encourage *deva* worship because they gradually elevate their followers, one who wants pure love of God should worship Kṛṣṇa in any ritual where *deva* worship is suggested.

The Position of Śiva

In his commentary on Sanātana Gosvāmī's *Bṛhad-bhāgavatāmṛta* (1.2.86), Śrīla Prabhupāda's disciple Gopīparaṇadhana Dāsa, drawing on Sanātana Gosvāmī's own commentary, writes, "The *Padma Purāṇa* includes... a list of ten offenses against chanting Lord Viṣṇu's names. Therein it is said, 'One who sees differences between any of Lord Śiva's qualities and names and those of Śrī Viṣṇu is an antagonist to *hari-nāma.*' Lord Viṣṇu cannot tolerate offenses against Lord Śiva, because Lord Śiva is the greatest of Lord Viṣṇu's empowered incarnations. Lord Śiva is especially empowered to distribute in the material world the elevated tastes of pure devotional service."

Lord Śiva is unique among the *devas.* He is an incarnation of Kṛṣṇa, but he is somewhat different from Kṛṣṇa, as yogurt is milk but not milk. He possesses qualities beyond those of any living entity and has an eternal dominion beyond matter. But to think that the name and personality of Śiva are equal in every way to those of Kṛṣṇa is offensive. And it is also offensive to see them as different.

The perfect way to reconcile the positions of Śiva and Kṛṣṇa is to worship Śiva as a changed incarnation of Kṛṣṇa who considers himself Kṛṣṇa's devotee and servant. In His incarnation as Śiva, Lord Kṛṣṇa acts as all-destructive time and as the father of all living beings. As Kṛṣṇa, He is aloof from matter; as Śiva, he consorts with the personified material energy. When we properly worship Kṛṣṇa, Śiva is included and pleased. But if we worship Śiva other than as a Vaiṣṇava, Kṛṣṇa's devotee, then neither is Śiva fully satisfied nor is Kṛṣṇa properly reverenced.

Chanting Without Any Form of This Offense

There are many names of God and many paths to Him, as well as paths and names that lead elsewhere. Various airline companies and routes may take us to Tokyo. If en route to Tokyo we think that we're flying on the only plane going there, or even with the only airline, we deceive ourselves in pride. Yet not every plane traversing the earth at this moment is headed for Tokyo, or even Japan, and some airlines don't have flights to the Far East at all. Of the airlines that do go to Tokyo, some have more direct routes, better service, or lower prices.

One who carefully studies the science of *bhakti,* devotional service to Kṛṣṇa, which involves the practice of chanting Hare Kṛṣṇa, will quickly understand that this route to love of God is direct. The flight includes ample in-flight service, and the price is only sincere eagerness. For our chanting in *bhakti* to be effective, we must distinguish between worship of the Absolute and the relative, while honoring all forms and names of the Absolute. Then our chanting of Hare Kṛṣṇa will quickly bring us to realization of our self and our sweet relationship with the one, all-attractive Lord Śrī Kṛṣṇa.

CHAPTER 11

Progress to Pure Chanting

The transforming power of Kṛṣṇa's holy names acts automatically when we abandon offenses, illusions, weaknesses, and material desires.

For days I struggled with a high fever. My swollen throat and pounding ear denied me sleep. While clear soup was part of the doctor's prescription, I had no appetite for anything. My weak body couldn't fully assimilate the little I could eat, so although the food was healthful, it didn't give me much strength. But as my health returned with medicine and a special diet, regular meals started to not only taste good but give me much needed energy.

Similarly, when we begin the regulated practice of chanting the *mahā-mantra*—Hare Kṛṣṇa, Hare Kṛṣṇa, Kṛṣṇa Kṛṣṇa, Hare Hare/ Hare Rāma, Hare Rāma, Rāma Rāma, Hare Hare—we generally displease the holy name (which is identical to Kṛṣṇa) in many ways. The holy name, therefore, works to slowly bring us to a state of spiritual health, and once health starts to be restored, the holy name begins to give us the full sustenance of transcendent love for God.

Just as a master neglects an offending servant and shows mercy to a repentant one, so the holy name, if unhappy with

Sometimes the beginning of spiritual life feels like a great struggle with determination, but after a person becomes fixed in devotion, the path becomes very easy and joyful.

our actions, thoughts, and attitudes, may choose not to show His full power. There are a number of ways to offend the holy name. The Sanskrit term for these offenses is *aparādha,* which literally means "without devotional worship," the word for worship being *ārādhanam.*

It is because of these *aparādhas* and other unwanted things in our hearts (*anarthas*) that chanting the holy name may not always be inspiring and full of exultation. Rather, we may feel that we mostly struggle and sometimes stumble on the spiritual path. The scriptures repeatedly inform us that saying Kṛṣṇa's name once is sufficient to destroy all karmic sins and awaken pure, selfless devotion for the Lord. Yet while we can rightly refer to the chanting as scientific in that it produces predictable results, chanting is not a mechanical practice. Kṛṣṇa is a person with feelings. His incarnation in sound, His name, has to want to show Himself to a spiritual aspirant.

Anarthas engender lust, anger, greed, illusion, pride, and envy, as well as distress, illusion, hunger, thirst, old age, and death. But the worst effect of *anarthas* is slow or negligible spiritual progress, in spite of practices such as chanting Hare Kṛṣṇa. The plant of devotion cannot grow in the presence of *anarthas,* which act like salt in the soil. *Artha* means goal, and *anartha* means an unworthy goal or a hindrance to fulfilling a worthy one. There are four major categories of *anarthas:* illusion, material desires, weaknesses, and offenses, or *aparādhas.* All *anarthas* stem from our envy of the power and opulence of God, alongside the desire for our own recognition. *Anarthas* cause our material bondage and all concomitant misery.

How do we become infected with *anarthas*? They are the results of actions in this and previous lives. Even pious activities can produce *anarthas,* such as a desire for salvation or heavenly pleasure. Sometimes *anarthas* arise when we become distracted, as when our progress in *bhakti* inspires others to respect us and we delight in such admiration. And while offenses to the holy name are *anarthas* themselves, if not eliminated they produce the other types of *anarthas* as well.

Illusions

When I first became determined to devote my life to serving Lord Kṛṣṇa, my mother was aghast at my disdain for the ordinary goals of family, money, security, and career. At one point, sobbing, she declared, "But you're too young to be disillusioned!" She didn't understand that our illusions prevent us from the ever-expanding bliss of loving God. We think we are the body or mind rather than the soul. We may imagine God to be only all-pervasive light, neglecting His supreme personal feature. The material world may seem to be a place of pleasure, and we may mistake rituals, philanthropy, and so forth, for the process of spiritual perfection.

While these kinds of illusion are certainly obstacles, chanting Hare Kṛṣṇa along with receiving instructions from both scriptures and a bona fide guru will quickly awaken us to the reality of ourselves, God, nature, and spiritual life.

Weakness of Heart

Weaknesses are a more difficult *anartha* to overcome. Though desire for fame or recognition is the cause of all *anarthas,* it can also be classified as an internal weakness. To help us cut this weed at the root, Kṛṣṇa tells us we must do service—even menial service—for devotees of the Lord. Throughout Vaiṣṇava history, spiritual aspirants have received Kṛṣṇa's mercy through such service. King Pratapa-rudra worked as a street sweeper in front of Kṛṣṇa's chariot in the Rathayātrā festival. Īśvara Purī, Lord Caitanya's spiritual master, cleaned his invalid guru's bodily wastes. And Śrīla Prabhupāda's exemplary disciple Jayānanda Dāsa took garbage to the dump.

Envy is another of the heart's weaknesses. Instead of envying others, we should desire their welfare and share our spiritual wealth. Kṛṣṇa will also remain hidden from one who is deceitful or fault finding. A hallmark of saintly character is to concentrate on the good in others while honestly assessing one's own faults.

Material Desires and Attachments

Through absorption in Kṛṣṇa's wonderful form, qualities, and activities, we rid ourselves of the weakness of attachment to things not related to Him. These include not only objects that may attract us, but also seemingly worthwhile goals such as heavenly comforts, mystic powers, and salvation. The story of Ulysses in Greek literature provides a useful analogy to our attempt to overcome material desires. Witches on a desert island would entrap sailors and devour them. When hearing the witches sing, the sailors envisioned them as enchanting beauties in a paradise. But when the sailors put in earplugs, they saw the reality and rowed quickly away. Similarly, chanting Hare Kṛṣṇa blocks our ears to the siren song of mundane pleasures. Knowing them as ultimate sources of misery and death, one easily gives them up.

A hallmark of saintly character is to concentrate on the good in others while honestly assessing one's own faults.

Offenses

The chanting of Hare Kṛṣṇa, Hare Kṛṣṇa, Kṛṣṇa Kṛṣṇa, Hare Hare/ Hare Rāma, Hare Rāma, Rāma Rāma, Hare Hare will gradually but quickly eradicate the three types of *anartha* I've discussed: illusion, weakness of the heart, and material desires. The fourth type of *anartha,* the *aparādha,* however, is a direct affront to the holy name. While constant chanting will destroy *aparādhas,* we also need to assiduously avoid them. If we make no effort to be free of the *anarthas,* and particularly the offenses to chanting, then the holy name won't give us mercy. Ultimately, only through Kṛṣṇa's mercy do we realize that the name is identical with the Lord Himself. In any form, including His holy name, Kṛṣṇa reveals Himself or not, as He desires. Our own efforts to evoke His mercy are necessary, but never sufficient.

The offenses to chanting are to offend other devotees of the Lord, to consider Kṛṣṇa's name to be equal to the name of some ordinary being, even a demigod, to disobey the spiritual master's order, to blaspheme scripture, to interpret the Lord's holy name in a mundane way, to think the glories of the holy name are exaggerated, to intentionally sin with the idea that chanting will erase the sin, to consider chanting the holy name to be material piety, to convey the name's glories to the faithless, to chant without attention, and to chant without faith and while maintaining material attachments.

A person free from these offenses is eligible to relish and rejoice in the pure name of Kṛṣṇa. Of course, even when chanted with offenses the holy name remains pure. One's *anarthas* only make it look impure, just as a colored filter makes a white light seem colored. A devotee of Kṛṣṇa in whose heart there remains only a tinge of *anarthas,* like the scent of perfume in an empty bottle, begins to feel the bliss of humility born of material detachment. Steady in his or her effort in serving Kṛṣṇa, the devotee finds chanting and other service to be easy. In a heart free of false ego, one feels compassion without envy and with respect for everyone.

Automatic Results

Up through the stage of freedom from *anarthas,* we have to struggle very hard, with determination, and then automatically everything will come. For example, steadiness in offenseless chanting automatically brings liberation. We lose the load of illusory identification and desires we unconsciously carry, and we feel truly free. Upon attaining this stage the relief is so great that we may think there is no greater gain. This inner detachment, along with steady devotion to Kṛṣṇa, brings freedom from all material miseries. But this is just the beginning of the life of spirit. From the platform of freedom, chanting Hare Kṛṣṇa brings one to such pleasure in spiritual life that one is keen for all service to Kṛṣṇa. Gone are all fatigue or boredom in such service, as experienced when the heart is full of *anarthas.*

At this stage of ecstasy, the physical aspects of chanting become automatic and unnoticed as the holy names dance within the mind. Naturally Lord Kṛṣṇa's qualities, form, and divine play blossom in the heart, the name as the catalyst. To chant the names like this is to know love and sweetness beyond anything else, material or spiritual.

In the lower stages one tends to think of mundane things while chanting, without understanding how the mind became distracted. But in the advanced stages of chanting, attachment to Kṛṣṇa awakens, and one's mind spontaneously runs to thoughts of Him.

Through chanting, this attachment deepens to overwhelming emotion, the flower that will produce the fruit of pure love. Such emotion arises in a devotee who is far past the stage of neutrality regarding desires and feelings for anything of the world. Materially, a great person subdues emotions with intelligence. The devotee surpasses the perfection of this art and feels spiritual emotions that are the pure prototypes of all worldly feelings.

As spiritual emotions mature into pure love of God, the chanting of Hare Kṛṣṇa reveals our original transcendent form, name, and relationship to the Lord. Even while the external life and affairs of the body continue, the soul within travels to Kṛṣṇa's kingdom to enjoy a life of which this ordinary existence is merely a twisted shadow. At the body's demise, one no longer returns to this world of birth and death, but attains the Lord's eternal, self-illumined abode.

Bibliography

Bhaktivedanta Swami Prabhupāda, A.C. (1970). *The Nectar of Devotion.* Los Angeles, CA: The Bhaktivedanta Book Trust.

Bhaktivedanta Swami Prabhupāda, A.C. (Trans.). (1972-8). *Śrīmad-Bhāgavatam.* Los Angeles, CA: The Bhaktivedanta Book Trust.

Bhaktivedanta Swami Prabhupāda, A.C. (1975). *The Nectar of Instruction.* Los Angeles, CA: The Bhaktivedanta Book Trust.

Bhaktivedanta Swami Prabhupāda, A.C. (Trans.). (1983). *Bhagavad-gītā As It Is.* Los Angeles, CA: The Bhaktivedanta Book Trust.

Bhaktivedanta Swami Prabhupāda, A.C. "Collected Lectures."

Bhaktivinoda Ṭhākura. (1998). *Śrī Bhaktyāloka.* (Trans. unknown). Badger, CA: Torchlight.

Bhaktivinoda Ṭhākura. (1999). *Śrī Bhajana-rahasya.* (Puṇḍarīka Vidyānidhi Dāsa, Trans.). Vrindavan, IN: Vrajraj.

Bhaktivinoda Ṭhākura. (1999). *Śrī Harināma Cintāmaṇi.* (Sarvabhāvana Dāsa, Trans.). Vrindavan, IN: Rasbihari Lal & Sons.

Bhaktivinoda Ṭhākura. (2002). *Śaraṇāgati and Gītāvalī.* (Daśaratha Suta, Trans.) [*The Songs of Bhaktivinoda Ṭhākura*]. Union City, GA: Nectar.

Bhaktivinoda Ṭhākura. (2008). *Jaiva Dharma.* (Sarvabhāvana Dāsa, Trans.). Los Angeles, CA: The Bhaktivedanta Book Trust.

Kṛṣṇadāsa Kavirāja. (1996). *Śrī Caitanya-caritāmṛta.* (A.C. Bhaktivedanta Swami Prabhupāda, Trans.). Los Angeles, CA: The Bhaktivedanta Book Trust.

Rūpa Gosvāmī. (2007). Padyāvalī. (Kuśakratha Dāsa, Trans.). Vrindavan, IN: Rasbihari Lal & Sons.

Sanātana Gosvāmī. (2011). *Śrī Bṛhad Bhāgavataāmṛta.* (Gopīparāṇadhana Dāsa, Trans.). Los Angeles, CA: The Bhaktivedanta Book Trust.

Viśvanātha Cakravartī. (1993). *Madhurya Kadambini.* (Deena Bandu, Trans.). Union City, GA: Nectar.

Viśvanātha Cakravartī. (2007). *Rāga Vartma Candrikā.* (Sarvabhāvana Dāsa, Trans.) [*The Bhakti Trilogy*]. Vrindavan, IN: Rasbihari Lal & Sons.

About the Author

Born in 1955 in New York City, Ūrmilā Devī Dāsī (Dr. Edith Best) joined the International Society for Krishna Consciousness in 1973 in Chicago. That year she became a disciple of His Divine Grace A.C. Bhaktivedanta Swami Prabhupāda. She had several occasions, along with her family, to meet with him personally. She and her husband, Pratyatoṣa Dāsa, have three married children and twelve grandchildren. Pratyatoṣa Dāsa and Ūrmilā Devī Dāsī have lived as *vānaprasthas* since early in 1996. She lives under the protection of her sons.

Ūrmilā has a Bachelor's of Science from Excelsior College (of the University of the State of New York) in Religion and Education, and Master of School Administration (MSA) and Doctor of Education in Educational Leadership from the University of North Carolina at Chapel Hill.

She has been an associate editor of *Back to Godhead* since 1990, a primary and secondary teacher for 27 years, school principal for 18 years, and is a member of the Sastric Advisory Council to the Governing Body Commission of the International Society for Krishna Consciousness.

Her other publications include *Vaikuṇṭha Children*, a guidebook for education in ISKCON; *Dr. Best Learn to Read,* an 83 book complete literacy program with technology enabling the story books to speak in 25 languages at the touch of a special "pen" (available from illuminationeducation.com and from krishna.com); and dozens of articles in *Back to Godhead.*

Ūrmilā travels internationally to teach about spiritual life, education, and leadership.

CPSIA information can be obtained
at www.ICGtesting.com
Printed in the USA
LVHW022330160820
663351LV00017B/2392

9 781494 297657